Alexander Ostrovsky

Ostrovsky (1823–1886)
in Russia. He wrote fo
His acknowledged mas
and *The Forest* (1871)

Alan Ayckbourn

Born in London in 1939, Alan Ayckbourn spent most of
his childhood in Sussex and was educated at Haileybury.
Leaving there one Friday at the age of seventeen, he went
into the theatre the following Monday and has been
working in it ever since as, variously, a stage manager,
sound technician, lighting technician, scene-painter, prop
maker, actor, writer and director. These last two talents
he developed thanks to his mentor, Stephen Joseph,
whom he first met in 1958 upon joining his newly
formed Studio Theatre Company in Scarborough.
A BBC Radio Drama Producer from 1965 to 1970,
upon the early death of Stephen Joseph he returned to
Scarborough to become the company's Artistic Director.
He holds the post to this day, though the theatre is now
named after its founder. He is the author of over fifty
plays, most of which received their first performance at
this Yorkshire theatre where he spends the greater part
of each year directing other people's work. More than
half have subsequently been produced in the West End,
at the Royal National Theatre or at the RSC. They have
been translated into over 30 languages, are seen on stage
and television throughout the world, and have received
many national and international awards. Alan Ayckbourn
was appointed a CBE in 1987 and in 1997 received a
knighthood for services to the theatre.

ALEXANDER OSTROVSKY

The Forest

a new version by
Alan Ayckbourn

from a literal translation
by Vera Liber

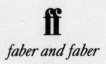

faber and faber

First published in 1999
by Faber and Faber Limited
3 Queen Square, London WC1N 3AU

Typeset by Country Setting, Kingsdown, Kent CT14 8ES
Printed in England by Mackays of Chatham plc, Chatham, Kent

A CIP record for this book
is available from the British Library

ISBN 0–571–20186–5

2 4 6 8 10 9 7 5 3 1

Characters

Raisa Pavlovna Gurmyzhskaya
a widow and wealthy landowner, 50s

Aksinya Danilovna (Aksyusha)
her distant relative, a poor girl of about 20

Yevgeniy Apollonych Milonov
Gurmyzhskaya's wealthy neighbour, about 45

Uar Kirilych Bodayev
Gurmyzhskaya's wealthy neighbour, about 60,
retired cavalryman

Ivan Petrovich Vosmibratov
a wealthy wood merchant

Pyotr
his son, early 20s

Aleksey Sergeyevich Bulanov
a young man of about 20

Karp
Gurmyzhskaya's servant

Ulita
Gurmyzhskaya's housekeeper

Gennadiy Neschastlivtsev
a travelling tragic player

Arkadiy Schastlivtsev
a travelling comic player

Act One

Morning. The hall and garden
of Gurmyzhskaya's country house.

Act Two

Afternoon. The forest.

Act Three

The following morning. The terrace and garden
of Gurmyzhskaya's house.

Act Four

That night. Another part of the garden.

Act Five

The following morning. Same as Act One.

Act One

Gurmyzhskaya's country estate, about three miles from the nearest important town.

A large hall. Upstage, two doors, one leading outside, the other into the dining room; stage left, a window and door into the garden; stage right, two doors, one into an inner room, the other into the corridor. Expensive antique furniture, three-leaved mirrors, flowers. By the window a working desk; stage left, a round table and several armchairs.

Karp, a servant, is standing by the door leading into the garden.

Aksyusha enters. She is about twenty, neatly but poorly dressed, little better than a housemaid.

Aksyusha Was Raisa Pavlovna asking for me?

Karp She certainly was, miss. Only the guests have arrived now, so she's gone in the garden.

Aksyusha (*taking a letter out of her pocket*) Listen, Karp, could you . . .?

Karp Could I what, miss?

Aksyusha Deliver this. To – you know who to.

She hands him a letter.

Karp Ah. Well. Now. Yes. I'd love to, but. Look at it this way. If I was to deliver this for you, you see, that could be my job, couldn't it? If she was to find out. I mean. Your aunt wants you to marry the other gentleman, doesn't she? Now if she caught me delivering this – Well.

Aksyusha (*apparently disinterested*) Suit yourself, then. (*She turns to the window.*)

Karp Well, alright, seeing it's you. (*He puts the letter in his pocket.*)

Aksyusha (*looking out of the window*) Has Raisa Pavlovna sold more of the forest yet, do you know?

Karp Yes, to Vosmibratov. We're selling the lot, don't ask me why.

Aksyusha Because she doesn't want her heirs to get anything, that's why. Once she's turned it into cash she can give it to anyone.

Karp That's as maybe. She's going a funny way about it, that's all I can say.

Aksyusha I've heard she wants the money for my dowry.

Karp God willing!

Aksyusha (*very seriously*) Indeed. God forbid!

Karp (*darkly*) Better you than that other lot, that's all I can say.

Aksyusha What other lot?

Karp That's not for me to say, miss. My lips is sealed.

Bulanov enters.

Bulanov (*to Karp*) Ah, Karp! Have you filled my cigarettes like I asked you?

Karp No, sir.

Bulanov Why the devil not? I distinctly told you to do it.

Karp Maybe you did. But when have I got the time to start filling cigarettes? I'm rushed off my feet, aren't I?

Bulanov I think you're getting above your station, Karp. I've a damned good mind to report you to Raisa Pavlovna.

Karp You report me, I'll report you for smoking, how about that?

Karp starts to leave.

Bulanov Look, I'm not going to speak to you again, Karp. It's about time you learnt to address people with a little more respect. Just because you're given a little latitude in this house, it doesn't mean you can – Karp. Come back here when I'm . . . talking to you. (*to himself*) Honestly! The man's absolutely impossible.

Karp has gone off. Bulanov stands frustrated. He sees Aksyusha for the first time, still gazing out of the window.

Ah!

He approaches and puts his hand on her shoulder.

Hallo.

Aksyusha (*startled, jumping away from him*) What on earth are you doing!

Bulanov (*startled in turn by her reaction*) Oh! I'm sorry!

Aksyusha How many more times? Don't do that.

Bulanov What did I do? What am I supposed to have done?

Aksyusha I've told you before. Don't – fiddle about with me. I don't come up and fiddle about with you, do I? Why does everyone insist on fiddling about with me? What do you think I am? Some sort of toy?

Bulanov It was only meant to be affectionate –

Aksyusha Well, don't do it. I'm a human being, leave me alone.

3

Bulanov I'm fond of you, that's all –

Aksyusha Well, that doesn't give you the right to creep up and prod me.

Bulanov It wasn't a prod, it was a pat. Why are you always so angry? Can't I even touch you?

Aksyusha No, you can't.

Bulanov I see. I might be all yours but don't touch, is that it?

Aksyusha I've told you before. I'm not all yours. I'm all somebody else's.

Bulanov Oh, come off it. I'm sick and tired of this. At this rate, you're going to ruin everything, you know.

Aksyusha I don't know what you're talking about.

Bulanov If your aunt wants us to marry –

Aksyusha – she can forget it –

Bulanov – no – then we get married. Or else. You'll be out on your ear and I'll be back home with Mother.

Ulita has entered furtively.

No, face the facts, if we don't – (*seeing Ulita*) What do you want?

Ulita I was just – looking for something, sir.

Bulanov Well, look somewhere else for it.

Ulita Yes, sir.

Ulita exits.

Bulanov Wretched woman, always prowling around. No, there's absolutely no point in being stubborn. Getting on your high horse. She's the one who pays the piper, the rest of us had better learn to jig.

4

Aksyusha There are some of us who can't be bought.

Bulanov (*scornfully*) Oh, bravo. There speaks one who's never been short of money in her life. Let me tell you something. Most people in this world get round to selling their souls sooner or later. And when they do, it's invariably for cash.

Ulita appears.

What do you want now?

Ulita I'm still looking for it.

Bulanov Well, buzz off.

Ulita exits.

Come on now. Why not be nice to me? When a thing's inevitable, the best thing to do is try and enjoy it.

Aksyusha You can't force me against my will, Aleksey Sergeyevich.

Bulanov No need. You'll come round, sooner or later. I can wait. You're not going to wriggle out of it, you know. I can wait.

Aksyusha (*quietly*) Then you'll be waiting a very long time.

She starts to leave, passing Karp in the doorway as she goes.

(*to Karp*) If Raisa Pavlovna asks, I shall be in my room. (*in the doorway, to Bulanov*) Please on no account attempt to touch me or speak to me again.

Aksyusha exits.

Karp Oh, dear, dear, dear.

Bulanov (*slightly irritably*) What?

Karp You're very young.

Bulanov I know I'm very young. What about it?

Karp It's not a good thing to be very young, sir. There's no advantage to be gained.

Bulanov What am I supposed to do about it?

Karp Keep on getting older, sir. It's the only way.

Bulanov Well, I've no doubt I will. But it takes time. Give me a chance, I've only just left grammar school.

Karp Grammar school! What good's that? There are those that hasn't been and gone to grammar school who are just as clever as those who have.

Bulanov Yes, but what are they clever at?

Karp They're especially clever at causing things to fall into their laps. They acquire the art of instinctual diplomacy.

Ulita appears from the corridor.

Oy! You. I've told you before. Get off out of it.

Ulita (*leaving*) Bastard!

She leaves.

Karp Excuse me. What were we saying? Oh yes. Now, why are you going around upsetting the young lady? What advantage is there in that?

Bulanov I wasn't, I was –

Karp You've got be more careful, you know. That Ulita's not creeping about for nothing. She'll pass it all on to the mistress. And she's not going to like it, is she? I mean, none of us knows what Raisa Pavlovna's got up her sleeve. She may be the mistress here, but she's still a bloody woman, isn't she? There's no way of knowing

6

what's on her mind. She changes it seven times a day, let alone a week. You follow me? I mean, here you are talking of getting married, but, maybe, she'll make you do something else! You're not even as free as you think you are. You were brought here because your mother was skint. And you can't afford to put a foot wrong, old son. My advice is to hold your breath, keep your mouth shut, your ear to the ground and your wits about you. Alright? Look out. She's here.

Karp exits swiftly. As Bulanov smooths his hair and twists his inadequate moustache, Gurmyzhskaya, Milonov and Bodayev enter.

Gurmyzhskaya (Raisa Pavlovna) is in her fifties, dressed modestly, almost as if in mourning. She carries a work box which is permanently with her.

Milonov (Yevgeniy Apollonych) is her wealthy neighbour, about forty-five, elegantly dressed.

Bodayev (Uar Kirilych), another wealthy neighbour, is about sixty, a retired cavalryman. He has short grey hair, a huge moustache and side-whiskers. He wears a black frock coat, tightly buttoned, adorned with medals. He walks with a stick and is a little deaf.

Gurmyz . . . no, I'm sorry, I'll say again, no one understands me, not a single soul.

Milonov I do . . .

Gurmyz Mmmm. Maybe.

Milonov Believe me, life is beautiful. Enjoy it while you can.

Gurmyz I believe you. I'm more than happy to believe you! Do sit down, gentlemen.

Bodayev (*muttering*) I'm sick to death of this conversation.

Gurmyz What was that?

Bodayev (*tetchily*) What? (*He sits away from them.*)

Gurmyz (*having noticed Bulanov*) Oh, Aleksis! There you are. Where on earth have you been hiding, dear? Gentlemen, may I introduce this young gentleman, Aleksey Sergeyevich Bulanov.

Bulanov (*bowing*) How do you do?

Gurmyz He's had a most interesting life, you know.

Milonov Really?

Bulanov Well, I wouldn't go so far as –

Gurmyz I must tell you about it. Aleksis, dear, go for a walk in the garden, would you?

Bulanov Oh. Righty-ho.

Bulanov exits. The others are now seated.

Milonov Relative of yours, is he?

Gurmyz No, he's not a relative. But surely it's not just relatives who have the right to our compassion.

Milonov No, no, no, indeed . . .

Gurmyz We're all of us responsible for one another, aren't we?

Milonov Absolutely, absolutely.

Gurmyz I mean, am I an island?

Milonov True, true . . .

Gurmyz Everything I own, my worldly possessions, all my money, belongs to the poor, doesn't it?

Bodayev Eh?

Gurmyz I'm only looking after it while I'm here – you and I, we're only custodians. The true owners of our wealth are every poor unfortunate person who ever walked this earth.

Bodayev If they want any money out of me they're going to have to wait till I'm dead. I'm not paying them a penny.

Gurmyz Not paying who?

Bodayev They can whistle for it.

Milonov Who can? (*to Gurmyzhskaya*) He's getting deafer, you know . . . (*to Bodayev*) Who are you talking about?

Bodayev This newfangled district council. They can whistle. It's daylight robbery.

Gurmyz (*loudly*) Why don't you move a little closer? Then you can hear us.

Bodayev Hang on, I'll move over there. I'll hear you better. (*He does so.*)

Gurmyz I was going to tell you, that young man, gentlemen, is the son of one of my oldest friends. We'd quite lost touch and then last year we met up again in St Petersburg. Years ago we used to be terribly close – virtually sisters. But then we both went our separate ways. I was widowed, and then a little later she got married. I begged her not to – having been through the whole business myself. At that stage, after all I'd been through, I'd developed a positive allergy to married life.

Bodayev To married life but not to men, I trust?

Milonov Uar Kirilych, really! Quite unnecessary!

Bodayev Only asking.

Gurmyz (*light-heartedly*) Most particularly to men like you.

Bodayev Quite right! I don't blame you. I'd do the same with mine.

Gurmyz Oh dear, he can't hear a thing, can he?

Milonov Raisa Pavlovna, as I've said before, you're a model for us all. Your modest life-style, your strong moral fibre, your virtuous example – you enrich our very air . . .

Gurmyz (*modestly*) Well . . .

Bodayev It's true. Six years ago, when we heard you were coming back to live on your estate, we were all absolutely terrified; wives made it up with their husbands, children with their parents; in some homes they even began talking in whispers . . .

Gurmyz Oh, go on with you! You can joke! Joke away if you must. Do you really think that I achieved this reputation without making sacrifices? Without a struggle? But we digress. By the time my friend and I met again in St Petersburg, she had long since become a widow too and, of course, had deeply regretted that she hadn't heeded my advice. With her eyes brimming with tears, she introduced me to her only son. A boy, who had just come of age.

Bodayev Ready for the army.

Gurmyz No, you mustn't judge from outward appearance. The poor boy is very delicate. And that held him back at school most dreadfully. He lagged behind his classmates. At grammar school he'd grown a moustache and he was barely out of the fourth form. And by then, of course, girls had started to show an interest in him and his mind was on – completely unsuitable things –

and there he was sitting among a load of twelve-year-olds. So humiliating for him. He got bored, became withdrawn, started walking the streets at night . . .

Milonov Oh, dear.

Gurmyz He suffered, his mother suffered; she didn't know which way to turn. She'd sold everything to have him educated, in the hope that eventually he'd get a good degree and be able to support her, but as time went on he lost the will to study at all. So I decided to do three good deeds at once.

Milonov Three?

Gurmyz To reassure the mother, to give the son a proper future and to get my niece settled.

Bodayev That's three.

Gurmyz I've brought the young man here for the summer; I'll let them get acquainted; then I'll marry them off and settle a good dowry on my niece. And that, gentlemen, is all there is to it. I believe there have been one or two rather malicious rumours and I'm hoping you will help dispel them.

Milonov Rumours? Really? How do you mean? (*realising*) Oh, I see. Surely not, who would dare . . .?

Bodayev People are people. You'll never stamp them out. No law against them. Unfortunately.

Gurmyz Not that I trouble myself too much over public opinion; I do good and I shall carry on doing good. Let them talk. You know lately I've been haunted by this terrible premonition, by the thought that very soon I shall be dead.

Milonov Nonsense!

Gurmyz No, the point is that in my dream I wish to die. I long for death.

Milonov What rubbish! You must live, my dear lady, you have so much more life left to live!

Gurmyz No, no, I don't believe I have . . .

Milonov Don't you dare die. You'd leave the rest of us devastated.

Gurmyz Maybe not today or tomorrow, but I'm convinced it could be soon. That is why I'm anxious to fulfil my duty as regards my heirs. Gentlemen, I need your advice.

Milonov Delighted to be of service.

Bodayev What's that?

Gurmyz As I've told you, I hope to settle my niece within my lifetime. My other nearest relative is my husband's nephew. I haven't seen him for fifteen years, nor have I had any news of him; but he's alive, that I do know. Now, there'd be no obstacle to making him my sole heir, would there?

Milonov I don't think so.

Bodayev Absolutely none.

Gurmyz That's what I thought, thank you. He never forgets me; every year he sends me these little gifts. I never know where he is so I can't write back to thank him. I feel faintly guilty. On top of that one of his father's debtors paid me back an old debt; only a small sum but all the same it worries me that I can't pass the money on to him. It's almost as if he's hiding from me. He seems to be all over the place. Archangel, Astrakhan, Kishinyov, Irkutsk.

Milonov What's he do for a living?

Gurmyz I don't really know. I was going to put him into the army. He was only fifteen when his father died and he had no real position in life. I was quite young myself then, but, from then on, I brought him up in accordance with my own firm moral precepts. I gave him a simple but strict education; what we called a poor boy's schooling; not because I was mean – but because of the principle. I am quite convinced that simple, uneducated people are always happier.

Bodayev I don't know about that. I don't believe an inadequate education necessarily guarantees you anything, least of all happiness.

Gurmyz Well, he's never complained about his upbringing; on the contrary, he even thanks me. I'm not against education, you understand, but nor am I entirely in favour of it. It seems to me that bad manners are the result either of total ignorance or excessive education. Good manners are the result of something midway between.

Milonov (*laughing*) Bravo!

Gurmyz I wanted my nephew to experience the school of hard knocks; a firm schooling, then into the army.

Bodayev Nothing wrong with that.

Gurmyz I sometimes sent him money, but, I must admit, only a very, very little.

Bodayev And, naturally, he began stealing.

Gurmyz No, no. On the contrary. Just look what he wrote to me. I always carry this letter with me.

She takes the letter out of the box and hands it to Milonov.

13

Read it, Yevgeniy Apollonych!

Milonov (*reads*) 'My dear aunt and benefactress. As befits my current circumstances, I write to you mortified by my own wretched shortcomings yet nonetheless not in total despair. Oh, quirk of fate! Held back by lack of education, shown up in front of my friends, I could see nothing ahead of me but the abyss of failure . . .'

Bodayev Not very complimentary to either of you, so far . . .

Gurmyz No, listen, carry on . . .

Milonov 'But I am not afraid! I know now that fame and fortune await! Although your miserable charity brought me to my knees on more than one occasion, to the brink of poverty and starvation, notwithstanding I kiss your hand. All through my childhood, throughout my adolescence, I had no strong ambitions but now everything is clear . . .'

Bodayev He writes alarmingly like a tax inspector . . .

Karp enters under the next.

Gurmyz It's not the words that count. It's the beautiful, unspoilt feeling . . . Yes, Karp, what is it?

Karp Ivan Petrovich Vosmibratov is here with his son, ma'am.

Gurmyz Oh. Would you both mind if I brought a tradesman in here?

Bodayev Be careful, he's a total rogue.

Gurmyz No, you can't say that, he's a wonderful family man.

Bodayev He might be a family man, but he's still perfectly happy to cheat everyone else.

Gurmyz I don't believe that.

Karp It's true.

Gurmyz (to *Karp*) That will do, Karp! Send them in.

Karp exits.

Milonov No, I agree with you, my dear. You're quite right. As you know, I'm a fierce defender of the family and family values. Ask yourself, Uar Kirilych, when were people happiest? When they lived in trees. It's a great tragedy that we've moved so far from the simple life that family relationships, our paternal responsibility for our lesser brethren, has more or less vanished. What's needed is a disciplined mind and a generosity of spirit. That's the right balance. Now look at us. Ever since the emancipation, we're hidebound by so many cold rules and clinical regulations we barely acknowledge each other any more. In the old days, it may have been rough and ready but at least there was warmth. Why do we need all these laws? You can't legislate for human relationships, can you? Let the heart decide. Let's all take responsibility for our own actions just for once. That's where the real rule of law is, here inside all of us.

Bodayev That'd work perfectly well if everyone was honest. But they're not. Most of them are complete and utter crooks.

Vosmibratov, a merchant, enters. With him is Pyotr, his son.

Gurmyz Come in.

Vosmib Thank you, ma'am.

Gurmyz Do sit down.

Vosmib Thank you. (*aside to Pyotr*) Sit down, son.

Pyotr sits by the door on the edge of a chair.

Milonov May I finish this letter?

Gurmyz Read on, they don't mind waiting.

Milonov (*reads*) 'Necessity, you inscrutable mother of invention! –'

Bodayev – there he goes again –

Milonov '– I thank you, thank you. Soon my name will be immortal, and so will yours, dear aunt. It will ring through posterity, through generations of children and grandchildren. Once again, I thank you for everything, Your humble servant, your nephew, child of nature, nurtured by misfortune, Gurmyzhskiy.'

Gurmyz (*taking the letter*) Thank you, Yevgeniy Apollonych! Now, let's ask this man of the people, shall we? Perhaps he'll give us an honest opinion. Ivan Petrovich, do you consider this letter well written?

Vosmib First class, ma'am! Just like a letter of application, couldn't be better.

Milonov But it's twelve years old. What's happened to your nephew since, with all his fame and glory?

Gurmyz I've told you, I don't know.

Bodayev Give him time. He may surprise you.

Gurmyz Whether he does or not, I am proud of this letter and quite overwhelmed by his gratitude. I have to say it, I love him very dearly. Perhaps I can persuade you both, gentlemen, to have lunch with me the day after tomorrow? The will should be ready for signature by then. I'm hoping you'll agree to witness it?

Bodayev I'll be here.

Milonov Everything will turn out for the best, believe me.

Gurmyz I suppose, to be painfully honest, I do have a bit of a guilty conscience as regards my heir. I've already sold off some parts of my estate.

Vosmib You've done quite enough for him already, my lady. On top of that you've given him the pleasure of living in capital cities.

Gurmyz I do help very generously. I'm never mean to those closest to me.

Vosmib Dead right. And if it benefits you as well, why not? You've earned it, I say.

Gurmyz I think you'll find that for the past seven years, I've had a very restrained lifestyle.

Vosmib Absolutely, ma'am. And may I say, as regards the rumours concerning your . . . I mean, in my book, your sheet is clean.

Gurmyz As I hope it always has been. That wasn't at all what I was saying. What I meant was, these days I live very economically.

Bodayev Listen, don't take this the wrong way, I'm not talking about you, but women have destroyed more estates round here than I care to mention. I mean, if a man squanders all his money there's usually some point to it, but a woman generally goes completely barmy. If she decides to give her lover a dressing gown – she sells a whole forest to pay for it. Usually to the first swindler that hoves into view.

Vosmib Quite right, your honour. My father used to say, when a woman's given her head, the first thing she generally does is lose it, eh?

Milonov (*to Vosmibratov*) Oh, Vanya, Vanya, you're so coarse!

Vosmib Little bit of truth in that, sir.

Milonov No, you're mistaken, my friend. Estates are not ruined by women, but by too much freedom.

Bodayev Freedom?

Milonov Make no mistake, I myself am all for freedom; I strongly oppose repressive measures of any description. Of course, I mean for ordinary, decent people; for the morally immature they're essential. But what on earth's going to become of people like us, eh? Merchants bankrupting themselves, the nobility losing all its money . . . You'll surely agree it'll soon become necessary to limit everyone's expenditure by law. It will have to be determined by class or profession, naturally . . .

Bodayev You should write a paper and submit it. It's a very good time for papers. Everyone's writing them. Don't lose heart, there are far dafter ones than yours.

He gets up. Milonov, Vosmibratov and Pyotr follow suit.

Gurmyz Gentlemen, I shall expect you the day after tomorrow.

Milonov I look forward to it eagerly.

Bodayev Until then. Adieu!

Milonov Goodbye.

Gurmyz Goodbye.

Milonov and Bodayev exit.

Gurmyz Sit down, Ivan Petrovich!

Vosmib Thank you, ma'am. (*sotto to Pyotr*) Sit down, son!

Pyotr sits down, as before.

You wished to see me, ma'am?

Gurmyz Yes, I did. Have you brought the money?

Vosmib No, ma'am, I must confess, I didn't pick it up. If it's essential, you tell me and I'll fetch it for you tomorrow.

Gurmyz Please do. And make sure you bring it all . . .

Vosmib I most certainly will . . .

Gurmyz (*rummaging in her box*) How much was it now, I forget?

Vosmib Don't you worry yourself about that now . . .

Gurmyz One and a half thousand, wasn't it? (*rummaging in her box*) Where's that piece of paper? I haven't thrown it away, surely? I can't seem to find it.

Vosmib You have a good look for it, ma'am.

Gurmyz The problem is, you see, that's still not enough money. I need more. You wouldn't like to buy another strip of forest off me?

Vosmib You take my tip, why don't you sell all of it now. What are you saving it for? That forest, ma'am, believe me, is nothing but trouble. Full of poachers, vagabonds and peasants satiating their ill-gotten lust.

Gurmyz All the same, I'm not selling it all. What sort of an estate would I have without a forest? Certainly not. Maybe, in time . . . But would you be prepared to buy that strip nearest the town?

Vosmib Well, I haven't the money on me now, but, yes, I'll take it off your hands if you're offering a fair price.

I'll help you out. But, *entre nous*, I'd like to talk about other goods altogether, if you get my drift.

Gurmyz Sorry?

Vosmib You have a relative do you not, a young girl, not too well-off . . .?

Gurmyz My niece, yes. What about her?

Vosmib Well, you-know-who there caught a glimpse of her and that's the other reason we're here.

Gurmyz I have no idea what you're talking about. Who's you-know-who?

Vosmib Him there. My lad. Stand up, son.

   Pyotr gets up.

Gurmyz Him?

Vosmib Pyotr, ma'am. My lad. He's as thick as six pine cones but he's gone and took a fancy to her, you see. Now he's cheap to run and if you give him a few acres of forest of his own, he'd be satisfied. He'll stand on his own two feet once you got him started, no worry. Won't you, son?

Gurmyz Well, I'm – I am very grateful to you – both of you – but . . . I'm afraid she already has a fiancé.

Vosmib I see. I see. May I enquire who that would be?

Gurmyz Aleksey Sergeyevich.

Vosmib Aleksey Sergeyevich?

Gurmyz Yes.

Vosmib The one living here?

Gurmyz Yes.

Vosmib He's her fiancé?

Gurmyz Yes. I don't know what nonsense they're saying about him in the town but they should all know that he's her fiancé.

Vosmib (*to Pyotr*) Did you hear that? She's already got one, hasn't she? What you trying to do? Make a fool of me? Sit down! Wait till we get home.

Gurmyz It's not that I think you're unworthy of her. Don't think that. For a girl such as her believe me even your son is a distinguished match. She's quite unworthy of Aleksey, but there you are.

Vosmib I quite understand, ma'am. No offence.

Gurmyz Let's talk about the forest, shall we? So you'll buy that other little piece from me, Ivan Petrovich?

Vosmib I will if I can. It may be outside my price bracket, that's all, ma'am.

Gurmyz How do you know? You haven't heard the price. What are you prepared to offer me?

Vosmib (*thinking for a moment*). Would five hundred roubles be about right?

Gurmyz What? One and a half thousand for the other one, and only five hundred for this one?

Vosmib About right?

Gurmyz But this plot's much bigger.

Vosmib Dead right, ma'am, I'm sorry that was a reflex offer. That was me not thinking it through. You give me the fair price, then.

Gurmyz Well, at least two thousand.

Vosmib Two thousand.

Gurmyz At least. (*Pause. Unconvincingly*) You should know, I've already been offered that.

Vosmib Then my advice is to take it.

Gurmyz Yes, well, I would have done but I didn't want to offend you.

Vosmib (*implacably*) No offence taken, ma'am.

Gurmyz (*her nerve breaking*) Ivan Petrovich, before God, have you no shame? Here I am, a poor defenceless woman in this wicked, unscrupulous world trying to do business.

Vosmib I know. I sympathise. It's a terrible place to do business. I don't know what He was thinking of when He made it.

Gurmyz I need that money for a good cause, you know. The girl has come of age, she's not very bright and I need to get her settled during my lifetime. You're a father, you must understand. You have a daughter of your own . . .

Vosmib Little trollop . . .

Gurmyz Ivan Petrovich, please!

Vosmib Beg your pardon, ma'am.

Slight pause.

Gurmyz Alright, one and a half thousand.

Vosmib Not possible, ma'am.

Gurmyz Well, I refuse to discuss it any more. You ought to be ashamed of yourself, that's all I can say.

Vosmib It's really a bit out of my price bracket just at present. (*suddenly relenting*) But, well, seeing as it's you and you seen me alright before . . .

Gurmyz I do need the money tomorrow, though.

Vosmib Don't you worry, I'll bring it tomorrow. Whatever's due.

Gurmyz Do that, please. (*She rings the bell.*)

Vosmib You write me out a little receipt, if that'll make you happy, so you'll know you received the money in total.

Gurmyz You'll bring the full three thousand?

Vosmib Me, I'm not an educated man so receipts don't mean nothing to me. I can't read 'em, you see. That's why I bring my lad along so he can sign for me.

    Karp enters.

Anyway, we'll take our leave, ma'am. We'll both be on our way and see you tomorrow.

Gurmyz Goodbye.

Vosmib Goodbye.

    Vosmibratov and Pyotr exit.

Karp (*as he follows them*) You wanted to see the young lady, madam. She's waiting.

Gurmyz Send her in.

    Exit Karp.

Sullen, ungrateful girl. I don't know why I put up with her.

    Enter Aksyusha.

Ah! At last! Where on earth have you been hiding?

Aksyusha (*looking down, quietly*) You wanted to see me?

Gurmyz Yes. I wish to speak to you about . . . you know who I'm talking about. Now, just at present, it is my wish that everyone regards him as your fiancé, do you understand? But that is purely a public arrangement, you see? Privately, I have yet to make up my mind whether or not you're worthy of him at all. I have still to make my final decision, is that understood?

Aksyusha I hope you'll be asking me as well.

Ulita enters unobtrusively under the next.

Gurmyz I will ask you when I'm ready to ask you, don't be so impertinent, girl. Teaching me my business. As I say, at present I want everyone to think of him as your fiancé. But God help you if I ever catch you flirting with him or flaunting yourself in front of him, is that clear?

Aksyusha Flaunting myself? What are you talking about?

Gurmyz Oh, don't you play the innocent with me. I remember you as you used to be and don't you ever forget it, girl. A grubby little street urchin, off tobogganing with every small boy in the neighbourhood.

Aksyusha That isn't true. At the age of six, I was helping my mother with her work. Day and night. Yes, alright, at holiday times I went tobogganing with the boys. Why not? But I've been living with you since I was ten and I've always tried to behave as you've taught me . . .

Gurmyz Don't worry, I intend to keep a very strict eye on you indeed. You may be a relative but you're a very, very, very distant one. Remember that. And, in the end, blood will out.

Aksyusha Who needs a fiancé like him?

Gurmyz Don't be so stupid –

Aksyusha He's no good, he's not clever –

Gurmyz Nonsense! He's clever, he's good, he's educated – He's streets above you in all departments. Why he's – You're doing this on purpose just to annoy me, aren't you? He is my choice, my taste. How dare you turn up your nose at him! Do you realise the number of society ladies who'd give their eye teeth – ?

Aksyusha That doesn't say very much for them then, does it?

Gurmyz Nonsense! What do you know? You're just an ignorant little –

Aksyusha Yes, I may be. I may be an ignorant street urchin but I'm clever enough to see through him.

Gurmyz That is enough! I am ordering you –

Aksyusha I will not marry him. What's the point of this farce?

Gurmyz Farce! How dare you? Don't you forget, young lady, I feed you and I clothe you and if I want you to play out what you regard as a farce, then play it out you will. You have no say in the matter. He is your fiancé, you are his fiancée and that is the end of it. Now, you will go to your room and stay there. That is also an order.

Aksyusha (*looking into her eyes*) Is there anything else?

Gurmyz Nothing. Get out of my sight!

Exit Aksyusha.

Just you wait, my girl. I've had far cleverer ones than you dancing to my tune, don't you worry. (*to Ulita*) Come here!

Ulita Yes, madam.

25

Gurmyz Come closer! That's it. Now sit down. No, not on the chair, on the floor! That's it! Now, are you listening?

Ulita (*sitting on the floor*) I'm listening, ma'am.

Gurmyz You know me, Ulita, don't you? You know how strictly I like this house to be run?

Ulita Oh, I know, I do know, ma'am. How could I not know?

Gurmyz I don't trust Aksyusha, she's a sly, deceitful girl. She often meets with Aleksey Sergeyevich, I know she does. I don't want that to become a habit. When I'm present, of course she wouldn't dare, but I'm not always with them. They can meet in the garden, even in the house when I'm not here. So, what I'm asking you to do, Ulita –

Ulita Say no more, ma'am, say no more. (*She kisses Gurmyzhskaya's hand.*) It's a marvel how I always understand you, isn't it? I've been following them like a shadow, don't you worry. They don't take a step without me. Wherever they are, I am.

Gurmyz You clever thing, Ulita. Quite shrewd, aren't you?

Ulita Oh, I am, I'm shrewd, ma'am, shrewd, that's me. Yesterday I tore my dress to shreds, creeping through the bushes. Then I got stung all over crawling through the nettles. But I overheard everything they were talking about, you know, like between each other.

Gurmyz Well, never mind the dress. I've got masses, I'll give you an old one of mine.

Ulita (*mysteriously*) Only recently they met right here.

Gurmyz Recently? How recently?

Ulita That fool Karp managed to ruin it. But I still noticed a thing or two.

Gurmyz What did you notice?

Ulita Well, she was very affectionate towards him. And he was doing like this . . . (*Makes a gesture with her hand.*) . . . saying like – no – get away from me, you know.

Gurmyz Really? (*She considers.*) You're sure you're not mistaken?

Ulita No! He was even like this at one point! (*Gestures with her hand.*) See?

Gurmyz Good gracious!

Ulita As if . . . you know, he was saying that he wasn't interested, you know.

Gurmyz I can't believe this is true.

Ulita I swear, ma'am, I'm very observant about that sort of thing. As if he had something else on his mind. Or possibly someone . . .

Gurmyz Well, we won't go into that. I think you've said enough.

Ulita I'm conscientious, that's all . . .

Gurmyz Well, conscientious or not, don't start pretending you can read people's thoughts because you can't. You're simply talking nonsense.

   Silence.

Ulita, you and I are about the same age, aren't we?

Ulita No, I think I'm a little bit older than you, ma'am.

Gurmyz (*irritably*) Don't argue, we're the same age. If I say we're the same age, we're the same age.

Ulita Well, who's counting, eh, ma'am? We're both inconsolable orphans of life, ma'am, aren't we?

Gurmyz Inconsolable? You? That's not my experience. All that trouble we had with you and that – Until I put a stop to it. Anyway. Enough of that. We will draw a veil. Now, listen, Ulita! Tell me something. Be honest . . . you can speak frankly . . . When you . . . when you happen to see an attractive young man . . . do you ever . . .? Or doesn't it enter your head . . .?

Ulita My head?

Gurmyz That it might be nice to – nice to – fall in love.

Ulita What, at my age? Oh no, I'm past all that, ma'am, I'm too old for that . . .

Gurmyz You're not old! Stop saying that! We're the same age. Now tell me, truthfully. Do you? Do you have such thoughts?

Ulita If you're ordering me to . . .

Gurmyz Alright, I am ordering you.

Ulita Well, sometimes, yes, like in a dream . . . (*tenderly*) . . . It floods over me. It starts here and then it . . .

Gurmyz Oh, don't be so disgusting. Go away!

Ulita moves away to the door but then lingers.
Gurmyzhskaya goes to the window.

Yes, he's not a bad-looking boy! He certainly made a good impression on me. The minute I set eyes on him. Oh, I'm still so young – at heart! I know it, even when I'm seventy I'll still be falling in love . . . If it wasn't for my own innate sense of caution, good breeding . . . What am I saying, he hasn't even given me a second look? (*looking out again*) Oh, you divine man! Yes, iron self-control, that's what's important. (*turning and seeing Ulita*) Oh! Are you still here? Come along, then. If you're very good, I'll give you two dresses, how about that?

They both go off.

Act Two

Sunset. The forest; two narrow paths run from opposite directions. A signpost, pointing one way: KALINOV; *the other:* THE PEN'KA ESTATE, LANDOWNER MRS GURMYZHSKAYA. *A large tree stump, a small bush. Aksyusha comes out of the forest and sits down on the stump; Pyotr comes from the opposite direction.*

Aksyusha (*running to him*) Petya!

Pyotr (*kisses her*) How are things?

Aksyusha The same. A bit worse.

Pyotr I've heard things are better.

Aksyusha What do you mean?

Pyotr I hear you're to marry a gentleman. Someone posher who can talk other languages and knows how to behave himself proper and wears the latest fashions, not like me –

Aksyusha (*putting her hand to his mouth*) Don't say that! You mustn't say that, it's not true.

Pyotr Must be true, your aunt said it herself.

Aksyusha You mustn't worry. Please don't worry . . .

Pyotr You be straight with me, now. Whose are you? Mine or someone else's?

Aksyusha I'm yours, my darling, I promise I'm yours. No one can change that, I swear. No, there's something else going on here . . .

Pyotr I mean, she just come out with it. Dad had been, you know, going round the houses, dropping hints about me and you and then she told him bluntly: 'She's betrothed.' I felt like I'd been hit with a sledge-hammer. When we got home, Dad bawled me out for two hours, then he has a rest and has another go. 'You so-and-so,' he says, 'You made me look a right so-and-so in front of the lady.'

Aksyusha She'd get rid of me just like that, only she begrudges the money. What are we going to do? Your dad's still expecting a dowry, isn't he?

Pyotr Yes, he won't settle for less than three thousand. 'If I don't get three thousand for you,' he says, 'Then it's not been worth feeding you,' he says. 'Even if I have to marry you to a nanny-goat,' he says, 'It'll be one with money.'

Aksyusha There's nowhere I can find three thousand. You asked me whose I was. What about you? Who do you belong to, then? Aren't you your own man?

Pyotr Of course I'm not. I belong to someone else, yes. Same as everyone like us does. Everyone like us, anyway. How can I ever be my own man?

Aksyusha I'm sorry. Please, don't be unhappy.

Pyotr What's there to be happy about round this place? The bloody trees are happier than I am. Don't tell me you're happy, either.

Aksyusha I'm – nothing. That all stopped a long time ago. The only time I feel anything is when I'm with you.

Pyotr Well, you're lucky . . .

Aksyusha Oh, don't be a fool! How can you be unhappy when you're with someone who loves you like I love you.

Pyotr Why shouldn't you? You can't help yourself. I'm irresistible.

Aksyusha Oh, well, if you're going to behave like that, I'm going.

Pyotr I'm sorry, don't get angry. Sorry! God, my head's coming off my shoulders. I can't think straight half the time . . . I'm that confused. I feel like pulling the bloody thing off and throwing it away . . .

Aksyusha Listen, just concentrate on us. Think about us. Think of me.

Pyotr I do. All the time. That's the trouble. I'm split in two. I'll just have to keep on at my dad, that's all. He'll get fed up of swearing at me eventually. He'll either bash my head in with a log, or he'll give in.

Aksyusha And then?

Pyotr Then we'll be away. I've got three hundred roubles of my own money; plus what I can nick from Dad's desk. We'll have money to burn.

Aksyusha Then what?

Pyotr Then – you and me, we're on a troika: 'Hey up, you beauties!' We arrive at the Volga – 'Whoa . . . whoa, there!' Then on to the steamer: sailing fast down river, you can't catch up with it along the bank. One day in Kazan, the second in Samara, the third in Saratov. Live as we please. Nothing but the best for us.

Aksyusha What if we met people you know?

Pyotr I'll screw up one eye like this. I'll look squint eye. Then no one'll recognise me. (*He demonstrates.*) See?

   She laughs.

I had to do that for three days once. Dad sent me to

Nizhniy on business, to keep me out of trouble. And when I'm there I meet these friends, you see, who persuade me to come to Lyskovo with them. Well, what am I going to do? Say no? On the other hand, if they find out about it back home, I'm in trouble. So what I do, I put on someone else's coat, and I wrapped up my face and I'm off. But on the steamer who should spot me but one of my dad's friends. And I thought, no, don't try and hide, just walk up to him, bold as brass. And I'm doing this and he's staring and staring at me. And he says, 'Would you mind telling me where you're from, young man?' And I said, 'Not at all. I'm from Myshkin.' Which I've never been to in my life. And he says, 'It's just that your face is somehow familiar,' he says. And I say, 'No, I'm not surprised, you know, because I'm often being mistaken for someone else.' But this bloke won't leave it alone, he keeps coming up to me, a second time, a third time, trying to place me. Well, I was getting a bit jittery by now. So in the end I said to him very loudly, in front of everyone, 'Do you know, I think your face is familiar to me. Didn't we spend some time in gaol together in Kazan?' Well, he couldn't get away from me fast enough. Like he'd been shot. That was funny!

Aksyusha And what happens when we've spent all the money?

Pyotr Oh, come on. One thing at a time.

She looks at him.

Well, we either come back and confess, or jump in the steepest, deepest ravine we can find and see whether we float or sink to the bottom.

Pause.

No, seriously, I'll plan it all out. Don't worry. Soon as Dad gets back, I'll start on at him. Pestering him.

33

Aksyusha Alright. And then we'll . . . We'll make a proper plan, won't we?

Pyotr Oh, yes.

Aksyusha Tell you what, come to the garden tomorrow evening. They all go to bed early in that house . . .

Pyotr Right.

They hear someone approaching.

That'll be Dad. You'd better go.

They kiss.

Aksyusha Goodbye, my darling.

Pyotr I'll see you soon.

They hurriedly go their separate ways. As they do so, from the depths of the forest Neschastlivtsev appears. He's thirty-five years old, but looks older, dark-haired, with a large moustache. Sharp, lively features, deeply lined, the result of a troubled and misspent life. He wears a long canvas coat, a wide brimmed hat and big Russian boots. In his hand, a thick, rough stick; on his back, a small suitcase, like a knapsack, with straps. He stops and sighs gloomily. Simultaneously, from the other direction, Schastlivtsev appears. He is in his forties with a face that seems almost rouged, hair like threadbare fur, a straggly moustache and a small beard. He wears a cravat, a short jacket, close-fitting trousers, coloured half boots and a peaked cap. Everything about him is worn and shabby. Over his shoulder, on a stick, hangs a very light shiny coat and a bundle in a coloured shawl. Both men are tired and breathing heavily. They meet.

Schast Aha!

Neschast (*gloomily*) Ah! Arkashka!

Schast The same, Gennadiy Dem'yanych, the self same.

Neschast Where to and where from?

Schast From Vologda to Kerch, sir. And you?

Neschast From Kerch to Vologda. Are you on foot?

Schast On my own two feet, sir. And you? Are you on foot?

Neschast No, I'm in a carriage and four, you idiot!

Schast I'm sorry, I . . .

Neschast Let's sit down, shall we?

Schast Oh yes. (*looking around*) Where shall we . . .?

Neschast (*sitting on the tree stump*) Well, I'm sitting here. You can sit wherever the hell you like.

Schast The ground. What's wrong with the ground?

Schastlivtsev sits down. Neschastlivtsev takes off his knapsack.

That's a highly unusual knapsack, sir.

Neschast Very useful. I made it myself, for touring purposes. Lightweight yet roomy.

Schast Excellent. Mind you, that's all very well provided you have something to pack in it. What have you got in there, then?

Neschast I have my suit, old chap. First-class fabric, made by a Jew in Poltava. When I was appearing at the festival at Ilinskaya, I had a number of suits made. There's also a top hat and a couple of wigs. And a fine pistol which I won from a wine merchant in a game of cards in Pyatigorsk. Only it's got a faulty firing pin so it's absolutely no use whatever. When I'm next in Tula I must get it mended. Sadly I no longer own a tail coat; I did have one, but I exchanged it for a Hamlet costume in Kishinyov.

Schast What on earth would you need tails for, anyway?

Neschast Of course I need tails, you fool. What if I'm in, say, Kostroma, doing a repertory season there. I may be invited to visit the governor or the chief of police, mightn't I? Or some other civic dignitary? It's alright for you comedians. You never get invited anywhere, anyway. But we legitimate actors, on the other hand . . . we're people to be reckoned with, you know.

Schast Oh, yes, indeed, I know only too well.

Neschast What have you got in your bundle, then?

Schast In here? A library, sir.

Neschast Extensive, is it?

Schast Thirty plays with their sheet music.

Neschast Any tragedies?

Schast Er – only two. The rest are mostly musical comedies or revue sketches.

Neschast Why do you carry all that rubbish round with you?

Schast Oh, it pays off. It's worth the investment, I assure you. I also have some small hand-props, medals, decorations, things like that.

Neschast Steal them, did you?

Schast I – obtained them. After they'd failed to pay our wages.

Neschast Where's your suit?

Schast This is it, I'm afraid. I haven't had a proper suit for a long time now.

Neschast How on earth did you get through the winter?

Schast Oh, I managed. True, it was hard occasionally, but necessity is the mother of spontaneous improvisation, as they say. On tour, they used to roll me up in the front cloth. When we reached the theatre they'd unroll me and as soon as the performance was over, they'd roll me up again.

Neschast Was it warm?

Schast Perishing. So you're off to Vologda, sir? There's no company there at present, you know.

Neschast You don't say? Well, there's no company in Kerch either, old chap. It folded.

Schast Really? Oh dear, then I'll move on. I'll go to Stavropol or to Tiflis, it's not too far.

Neschast The last time we met was in Kremenchug, wasn't it?

Schast In Kremenchug, yes.

Neschast When you were still playing juve leads. What happened to you after that, old chap?

Schast I decided to specialise in comedy. Bad mistake. The competition was frightening. All these educated people getting all the parts: retired civil servants, ex-army officers, university students – all desperate to get on stage. Your proper actor can't make a living at all these days. So I was forced to take up prompting, sir. What do you think that's like for a performer with a sensitive soul? A prompter! Life is a drain down which we all must flow, Gennadiy Dem'yanych, and for me it's blocked.

Neschast Serves you right. Any damn fool can be a comedian. No wonder they're all at it.

Schast Yes, but none of them are any good.

Neschast Of course they're not. They're killing off the business. Why on earth have you grown that beard?

Schast What?

Neschast It's dreadful. Call yourself a Russian? Looks like a tart's pubic hair. Either shave it off or grow a proper one.

Schast I've tried. I can't. It just sort of sprouts. Like feathers. You're quite right. I'll – shave it off. So, how's life with you, Gennadiy Dem'yanych?

Neschast Appalling.

Schast Oh, dear . . .

Neschast If you must know I had a bit of a set to with the producers back there. Actually came to blows. Well, you know me, old chap. I tend to say what I feel. I don't mince matters . . .

Schast No, you don't . . .

Neschast You see, if there's one thing I can't stand it's meanness. Meanness with money, meanness of spirit. The modern impresario puts no value on art, old chap. They're all petty, small-minded, penny-pinching accountants. I rather hoped things would be better up there in the north.

Schast Just the same, I'm afraid. Or so I found. I couldn't make a go of it.

Neschast You're not comparing yourself to me, I hope?

Schast (*offended*) Well, at least I'm not stupid enough to have blazing rows with managements.

Neschast (*threateningly*) What? What are you saying?

Schast (*backing away*) What I mean is – I don't pick fights. I'm more easy-going. I've never attacked any-one . . .

Neschast No, you always get beaten up instead, don't you? (*He laughs.*) Two sorts of people in this world. The beaters and the beaten. You pays your money . . . You, you let people walk all over you. Which town was it where that governor kept throwing you out? Remember that?

Schast Oh, not that again. It's all forgotten.

Neschast Forgotten? It's a living theatrical legend, old chap. How many – ? Three times they drummed you out of town. No sooner had they thrown you out of one gate than you came back through another. Finally, even the governor loses his rag: shoot him, he says, I'll take full responsibility. If he comes back once more, shoot the little bastard . . .

Schast (*uneasily*) As if they'd be allowed to shoot me!

Neschast No, true, they didn't shoot you, but the Cossacks did chase you for five miles, didn't they . . .

Schast Three, at the most.

Neschast Anyway. I must get on. Heaven knows where. To another life. I've finished with theatre, you know, Arkadiy!

Schast Oh, come now . . .

Neschast I shall miss it. That last performance, you should have seen me. How I acted! My God, how I acted!

Schast Good, was it?

Neschast Good? I was . . . Oh, what's the point of telling you? How could you understand? The last time I was in Lebedyan I finished my death scene, and who should be watching from the wings but the legendary Nikolai Rybakov himself. My lifeless corpse was borne hence on a litter and there he was waiting for me. He put his hand on my shoulder like this . . .

He drops his hand on Schastlivtsev's shoulder with some force.

Schast Oh, please . . .

Neschast It's alright, old chap. I'm only demonstrating to show you . . .

He puts his hand on Schastlivtsev's shoulder again.

Schast Please, do be careful . . . I have an old injury . . .

Neschast Injury?

Schast When I was working with Bichevkin. He was playing Lyapunov and I was Fidlyer. And during the rehearsals he says, 'Arkashka, I think it might be very effective in this scene if I picked you up by the collar and threw you out of the window.' I begged him on my knees, I said, 'Listen, I could get killed.' And all he says is, 'Don't be afraid, trust me, dear boy.' And then, just before the first performance he says, 'Put something down under the window for him to land on,' he says, 'So that I don't actually kill him.' Well, I'm convinced my end is nigh. And of course you know Bichevkin. As usual he gets completely carried away as soon as he gets in front of an audience. His eyes are bloodshot, his face is twitching, he's practically frothing at the mouth – he's demented. And he grabs me by the collar, swings me round his head – well, I blacked out, Gennadiy Dem'yanych – I flew through the air for about twelve feet, and broke the door of the ladies' lavatory. It's alright for you tragedians! He took thirty curtain calls for that scene; the audience were throwing the seats. I could have been crippled for the rest of my life.

Neschast Sounds a good bit of business. I must remember that. What did he do, exactly? (*He steps towards Schastlivtsev.*)

Schast (*retreating, alarmed*) No, no, please . . .

Neschast Well, another time. Where was I?

Schast Nikolai Rybakov . . . in the wings . . . you being borne hence . . .

Neschast Oh, yes. Anyway. I'd come off stage after my death scene and he's standing there in the wings and he puts his hand on my shoulder and he says: 'You,' he says, 'were born to die,' he says. (*Pause.*) I was very touched by that. (*Pause.*) Got any tobacco, have you?

Schast Tobacco? Sorry, not a speck.

Neschast How can you possibly go on the road with no tobacco? Ridiculous.

Schast You haven't got any either, have you?

Neschast I've had tobacco, laddie. I've had tobacco like you've never seen in your life. Don't try and teach me about tobacco.

Schast I wasn't.

Neschast 'You don't have any either.' How dare you say that to me? I just happen to have run out, that's all.

Schast Well, I've run out as well.

Neschast I don't suppose you've even got any money?

Schast Nothing at all.

Neschast No tobacco and no money. What are you? A monk?

Schast At least I can't get robbed. You wouldn't like to lend me some money, Gennadiy Dem'yanych?

Neschast I don't have enough for myself. Do you have any relatives or friends hereabouts?

Schast No. But even if I did, they wouldn't give me any money.

Neschast I have.

Schast Relatives? Ah . . .

Neschast I would have preferred to have passed them by. A matter of pride, you know. Though I could drop in, obviously.

Schast I do have an uncle, a shopkeeper, but he lives some little distance from here. I stayed with him once, but I . . .

Neschast What?

Schast Well, it was very unpleasant. To start with, when I first arrived, they wouldn't let me in at all. They just kept peering at me through a crack in the front door. Then, at last, my uncle himself comes out and he says: 'Oh, it's you.' Just like that. 'It's you, is it? What have you come for?' 'To visit you, Uncle,' I said. 'So you've given up making a howling ass of yourself, have you? Well, in that case, you can sleep in the box room. Only visit the baths first.' So I lived with them. Up at four o'clock, lunch at ten, to bed at eight. And no one in the house ever spoke, Gennadiy Dem'yanych. It was as if they'd died and nobody'd broken the news to them. All day Uncle's in the shop, and Auntie sits and drinks tea. She keeps looking at me and sighing and saying: 'You

poor unfortunate man, you've destroyed your own soul!'
In the end I got so depressed, I seriously considered
hanging myself. One night I just couldn't take it any
more. I ran away. That's relatives for you, brother.

Neschast Serve you right. Steer clear of relatives, old
boy. They're strictly for emergencies only. Mind you, I'm
so tired these days I could . . . What we need to do, you
know, is to start a company of our own.

Schast I thought you said you were giving it all up.

Neschast All we need to find is a good young dramatic
actress . . .

Schast I could be the manager . . .

Neschast That's the way forward. Only one snag. We
haven't got an actress. You know what I mean when I
say actress? One with life bubbling behind her eyes and
fire in her soul. Blazing!

Schast Well, you won't find one here. Not in the middle
of a forest. Too dangerous. (*He laughs.*)

Neschast Is that supposed to be a joke?

Schast Er – not particularly . . .

Neschast I'm talking seriously here.

Schast I'm sorry.

Neschast You vaudeville actors, all you can do is make
jokes. I'm talking about a woman who would throw
herself into a whirlpool for love – that's what I mean by
an actress. (*He reflects.*) Well, I must be on my way.

Schast Where to?

Neschast None of your business. Fifteen years since I've
been back, you know. I was practically born here.

43

Childhood memories, innocent games, dovecotes, all that
sort of rubbish . . . fond memories. Anyway, Auntie'll
be pleased to see me. She must be getting on a bit now.
Even according to female calculations, she'll be over fifty.
I haven't forgotten her. I still send her presents occasionally. Shoes, frozen salmon, bits of jewellery, a jar of brick
tea, cured fillet of sturgeon – I can't remember it all.
Of course it would be preferable for both of us to arrive
at the front door in a carriage for the servants to meet
us . . . rather than on foot, in rags. Oh, God! (*wiping
away a tear*) Curse this pride, Arkadiy, curse it! (*He puts
his suitcase on his back.*) Let's go. There's bound to be a
corner for you. Some box room or other.

Schast Excuse me, where are we going, Gennadiy
Dem'yanych?

Neschast Where? (*pointing to the sign post*) What does
that say?

Schast (*reading*) To the Pen'ka estate, owner Mrs
Gurmyzhskaya.

Neschast My wretched destiny leads us there. Your arm,
my friend. (*as they go*) *What should such fellows as I do
crawling between heaven and earth? We are arrant
knaves all . . .*

   Exeunt slowly.

Act Three

*An overgrown garden; at one side, a low terrace covered
in flowers. Three or four steps leading down.*

    *Gurmyzhskaya enters onto the terrace. Bulanov is in
the garden.*

Bulanov (*helping Gurmyzhskaya down from the terrace*)
Good morning, Raisa Pavlovna! (*He kisses her hand.*)

Gurmyz Good morning, my dear.

Bulanov (*showing concern*) How are you feeling,
ma'am?

Gurmyz Thank you for asking, I'm well. I feel
particularly lively, for some reason, despite the fact I
slept very badly. I had such unpleasant dreams. Do you
believe in dreams? There are some you can't get out of
your mind, can you?

Bulanov What did you dream?

Gurmyz I couldn't possibly tell you that. Some dreams,
maybe, but not this one.

Bulanov Why not, ma'am?

Gurmyz Well . . . if you tell someone your dreams, it's
like revealing one's secret thoughts or desires and that's
not always proper. I'm a woman, you're a man.

Bulanov What difference does that make, ma'am?

Gurmyz Oh, you're such an innocent. Well, if you must
know, I dreamt of you.

Bulanov Of me? I'm pleased to hear that, ma'am.

Gurmyz Really?

Bulanov That means you were thinking about me when you went to bed.

Gurmyz And that pleases you?

Bulanov How could I not be pleased, ma'am? I'm constantly terrified that you're going to get angry with me over something and send me back to Mother.

Gurmyz Oh, how silly! Why should I get angry with you? My poor boy, you're not frightened of me? Surely?

Bulanov I hear you can be very strict.

Gurmyz I'm glad you heard that. Yes, I can be. But not with you. I shan't be strict with you. I don't want you to be frightened of me, Aleksis.

Bulanov It might be easier if I knew . . .

Gurmyz What? If you knew what? Go on.

Bulanov How to please you.

Gurmyz Guess.

Bulanov I'm afraid I've no talent as a mind reader, ma'am.

Gurmyz No? Then what do you have a talent for, do you suppose?

Bulanov For anything you ask of me. I could manage the estate, organise the peasants . . . If only you still employed serfs, I could really have – Nevertheless, I may be young but you won't find a better manager . . .

Gurmyz Oh, that dream of mine! If only I could get it out of my head.

Bulanov Perhaps there's something worrying you?

Gurmyz Well, I can speak openly to you, surely. You see, I have a nephew.

Bulanov I know, ma'am. You love him very much. You often speak of him.

Gurmyz My dear, sometimes people speak of one thing but are thinking something quite different.

Bulanov You mean you don't love him?

Gurmyz It's not that I don't love him, but . . . How can I put it? He's superfluous now. I've got everything nicely sorted. I've decided how I'm going to dispose of my fortune. What if he suddenly turns up here now? How could I refuse him? I should have to give him a share, and deprive someone I love.

Bulanov Don't give it to him, ma'am.

Gurmyz I'd have to. How could I refuse him? He's done nothing wrong. What would people think of me if I turned away a blood relative? What if he's destitute? I'd have to support him. He'd probably want to make his home here. I couldn't throw him out.

Bulanov I'll throw him out, if you like.

Gurmyz (*in alarm*) Oh, God forbid! Do be careful! That's exactly what my dream was about. He came here and shot you dead before my very eyes.

Bulanov Well, I wouldn't set too much store by dreams, ma'am. My advice is not to think of him any more, or else you'll carry on dreaming about him.

Gurmyz I can't complain thus far, I suppose. I haven't clapped eyes on him in fifteen years. Personally I'd be delighted if it remained the same for another fifteen.

Bulanov Raisa Pavlovna, forget about him entirely. Otherwise, who knows, you might conjure him up.

Gurmyz Heaven forbid!

Enter Karp.

Karp Good morning, ma'am. Tea is ready, ma'am.

Gurmyz Come on, Aleksis!

Karp And to let you know, mistress, that the master arrived in the early hours.

Gurmyz Master? What master?

Karp Gennadiy Dem'yanych, ma'am.

Gurmyz (*in alarm*) Gennadiy Dem'yanych? Really? Did you hear, Aleksis? (*to Karp*) Where is he?

Karp I put him and the other gentleman in the summer house. I made their beds up there, ma'am. He said they'd stopped in a hotel in town and left all their luggage there. They came up on foot because they felt like a stroll.

Gurmyz What else did he say?

Karp He was a bit out of sorts, ma'am.

Gurmyz What do you mean, out of sorts?

Karp Like, a bit dazed, ma'am, probably from the journey, ma'am. He asked for paper and ink, walked about the summer house for a long time, having a think, sat at the table, wrote a note and told me to give it to you. (*Hands her the note.*)

Gurmyz What on earth is this? (*reads*)

> *My fate is cruel!*
> *How cruel the fates!*
> *When nothing but the grave awaits . . .*

48

What is this, Aleksis? I don't understand it at all.

Bulanov If you don't understand it, I certainly don't.

Gurmyz (*to Karp*) Is he still asleep?

Karp No, ma'am. Got up early to have a bathe, I think.
I haven't seen either of them this morning, ma'am.

Gurmyz (*shrugging her shoulders*) One shouldn't set too
much store by dreams, eh? Come on, Aleksis.

Exeunt. Pause.
*Neschastlivtsev enters, dressed smartly with a black
top hat. Following him is Schastlivtsev in his former
outfit.*

Neschast . . . no, you see, Arkadiy, my aunt is a fiercely
respectable woman, strait-laced even. I wouldn't want
her to know, old chap, that I'm an actor, and a
provincial one at that. So don't you dare let the cat out
of the bag. I am Gennadiy Dem'yanych Gurmyzhskiy, a
retired captain or major, or what-have-you. Anyway, a
gentleman, and you're my servant.

Schast What do you mean, your servant?

Neschast Just a servant, that's all. It merely means I
won't have to take you into the drawing room. I mean,
how could I present you to Auntie? She's a devout
woman, this is a quiet, God-fearing household, old chap.
Imagine how they'd react if you – er – well, with your –
and so on. No, with a face like yours, a servant is
absolute type-casting.

Schast A face like mine? What's wrong with my face?

Neschast Nothing wrong at all. It's a servant's face,
that's all. What are you complaining about? You'll get
fed, won't you?

Schast I'm not at all sure about this . . .

Neschast Stop bellyaching. Some of the finest actors in the world have played servants . . .

Schast But that was on the stage.

Neschast Well, then, pretend you're on the stage.

Schast No, I'm sorry. I positively refuse. I'm leaving. I still have some pride, you know.

Neschast You may still have pride but I bet you still haven't got a passport, have you?

Silence.

Have you? You haven't had one for at least twelve years to my knowledge. The only identification papers you carry is a bad review from the *Kursk Evening News*.

Pause.

Schast (*muttering*) It wasn't that bad.

Neschast I have only to blink, old chap, and you'd be deported like a common vagrant.

Pause.

Look, do it for me. As a friend, old chap!

Schast (*grudgingly*) Well, maybe as a friend, I might.

Neschast Listen, I'm not running down the profession, never imagine that for a minute. But it's damned awkward – a respectable house like this – let you loose, it'd be like the demon king popping up in the middle of *Swan Lake*. I know it'll be difficult but just try and behave like a decent servant, there's a good fellow. Quickly, take your cap off, someone's coming.

Enter Karp.

Karp How do you do, my dear master! Did you sleep well, sir?

Neschast Well enough, old chap, well enough.

Karp You look older, sir.

Neschast Life, old chap . . .

Karp Oh, I understand, sir. I've lived life. No need to tell me. In your case that'll be the military service . . .

Neschast Ah, yes. The old service militaire.

Karp Campaigns, no doubt?

Neschast (*with a sigh*) Oh, yes. Ceaseless campaigning . . .

Karp Lot of travel, sir?

Neschast You name it, I've fought there. How's life here?

Karp Here? Middle of a forest, nowhere to go, rooted to the spot. Might as well be a tree, if you get my meaning. Would you care to go in, sir? Your aunt's expecting you for tea.

Neschast (*moving to the terrace*) By all means. Listen, Karp, can you take care of my man there? Give him some tea, there's a good chap!

Karp I'll do that, sir.

    Neschastlivtsev goes indoors.

(*turning to Schastlivtsev*) Well, now . . .

Schast (*to himself*) Oh, God, he's not left me alone with him, has he?

Karp What's your name?

Schast Tartuffe.

Karp Eh?

Schast Tar – tuffe.

Karp Foreigner, are you?

Schast That's right. And yours?

Karp Karp Savel'ich.

Schast Carp?

Karp Karp.

Schast Never.

Karp True.

Schast A carp's a fish.

Karp No, that's carp. I'm Karp.

Schast What's the difference?

Karp It's spelt different, isn't it?

Schast Take my tip you'll change it to something more sensible. Cod for instance.

Karp Listen, do you want some tea?

Schast No.

Karp No?

Schast No.

Karp None at all?

Schast None at all.

Karp Why's that, then?

Schast Remember the old maxim:

> *If you want a life that's sweet,*
> *Always bathe before you eat;*
> *Always eat before you drink*
> *You'll live longer than you think.*

You'd do well to remember that, Perch.

Karp Karp. Food, then? I could ask the housekeeper . . .

Schast Bottle of vintage wine. In the summer house, there's a good chap.

Karp Wine? Well, I'll try, but . . .

Schast Have a go for us, Turbot.

Schastlivtsev exits.

Karp Karp! Where'd they dig him up from? Bloody jumped-up valet.

Enter Vosmibratov and Pyotr.

Oh, it's you. What do you lot want?

Vosmib We're here to see the mistress on business.

Karp Well, you'll have to wait. She's entertaining the colonel.

Vosmib Colonel?

Karp Her nephew, the colonel. Haven't seen each other for fifteen years.

Vosmib Will he be long?

Karp Long? He's here for good. I daren't interrupt.

Vosmib Fierce is he, this colonel?

Karp Like a bear with gout.

Vosmib We'll wait then.

Karp Very sensible.

The three go off. As they do so, Neschastlivtsev and Bulanov come out of the house.

53

Neschast I say, that's a very attractive cousin I have there . . .

Bulanov Aksyusha? Indeed, sir.

Neschast Take my tip and marry her, old chap, marry her!

Bulanov Would you approve, sir?

Neschast Me? It doesn't make a blind bit of difference to me. People are born, they marry, they die, it's all the same to me.

Bulanov Nonetheless, I'd like to think I had your approval, sir.

Neschast Why on earth do you need my approval? You're not going to marry me. No, what you're going to have to do is sweet talk my aunt into giving you both a proper settlement. She's a rich woman, you know. You're a shade young – but you might pull it off.

Bulanov I'm sure I can, sir. I'm very grateful to you, sir. Thank you.

Neschast (*studying him*) Yes. Bravo! Where did you learn all that so young?

Bulanov Learn what, sir?

Neschast What you've just been using on me, old chap. The gentle art of soft talk. Also known as social crawling.

Bulanov Hardship's a good teacher, sir.

Neschast Hardship? What do you know about hardship?

Bulanov I've had a tough upbringing, sir.

Neschast Nonsense, I don't believe it.

Bulanov My father left me very little.

Neschast What's very little?

Bulanov Not enough.

Neschast And what would you consider enough?

Bulanov Eight thousand acres and forty thousand roubles.

Neschast (*dryly*) Very reasonable.

Bulanov (*missing the irony*) Exactly, it's not much to ask, is it? The point is, I never had a proper education. I didn't even finish school.

Neschast Damn! That's a pity.

Bulanov Why?

Neschast Well, I was thinking of leaving you some money myself but if you're not properly educated, that's out of the question I'm afraid.

Bulanov Are you laughing at me?

Neschast Perish the thought.

Bulanov No, seriously, I need money. If you have money, what does education matter? If you have money, you don't need a brain at all, you can get along without one.

Neschast Smaller hat size as well.

Bulanov What?

Neschast You don't happen to have a cigarette on you, do you?

Bulanov (*taking out his cigarettes*) Yes, of course, I –

> *Gurmyzhskaya appears on the terrace. Bulanov, seeing her, puts his cigarettes away again swiftly.*

No. Sorry. I don't smoke.

Neschast You don't –?

Bulanov (*quietly*) Not at present.

Gurmyzhskaya comes down into the garden.

Gurmyz Do you know, Gennadiy Dem'yanych, I'd never have recognised you, you've changed so much. I'm so glad you didn't forget us entirely. We've talked about you nearly every day.

Neschast How could I ever forget you, Auntie?

Gurmyz That beautiful rosary you sent me. I think that was my favourite gift of all.

Neschast You know, whilst I was parcelling up that rosary, I thought: 'Good woman, take this in your hands and pray for me. *In thy orisons be all my sins remembered.*'

Gurmyz Each day, my dear, each day. Now, I haven't asked you about yourself. I gather you're no longer in the army?

Neschast No, no. One can only endure that much. Besides there's nobody left to fight at the moment. But oh . . . what a joy it was to wield the old sabre. Nothing like a good war! But the army in peacetime, that's a different kettle of fish entirely . . . you're just a glorified civil servant.

Gurmyz So you've changed your job?

Neschast I have indeed.

Gurmyz (*after a pause*) And – is it an enjoyable one?

Neschast Very rewarding, Auntie.

Gurmyz Yes. And presumably you're on holiday from – this job, at the moment?

Neschast Just for a few days. While they move things around.

Gurmyz (*mystified*) I see.

They appear to have exhausted this conversation.

Well, I'm delighted you dropped in. Are you comfortable in the summer house?

Neschast Nature, greenery, birdsong, seclusion! After the thunder of cannon fire, it's paradise for the soul.

Enter Karp.

Karp Excuse me, Vosmibratov has been waiting some time, ma'am.

Gurmyz Oh, goodness yes, I'd forgotten. I told him to come early. Send him here!

Exit Karp.

(*to Neschastlivtsev*) Would you excuse me. Perhaps you'd like to explore the estate. Aleksis can show you.

Neschast No, I walk only at night. Fear of sniper fire. Old habits die hard. (*to Bulanov*) Come along, old chap, we'll go to the summer house! I'll show you something, might amuse you.

Bulanov Alright, sir.

Exeunt. Enter Vosmibratov and Pyotr.

Gurmyz Do forgive me, I forgot all about our meeting.

Vosmib No matter, ma'am. I understand your nephew's arrived?

Gurmyz That's correct.

Vosmib Ah, well, I won't detain us, then.

Gurmyz No, we mustn't.

Vosmib Time and tide.

Gurmyz Absolutely.

Vosmib Let's get straight down to it.

Silence.

Gurmyz Did you bring the money?

Vosmib Of course.

Silence.

Gurmyz Well. May I have it?

Vosmib Ah! If you wouldn't mind . . .

Gurmyz What?

Vosmib Little matter of the receipt, ma'am. As promised.

Gurmyz Oh, yes, of course. Now where did I put it? I made out a fresh receipt especially. (*She searches in her box.*)

Vosmib (*only half joking*) Come along now! Come along! This won't do, will it?

Gurmyz (*somewhat flustered*) I had it! I know I had it!

Vosmib Call yourself a business woman. Dear oh dear! Come along, come along! Time is money!

Gurmyz (*finding it*) Here it is!

She hands him the receipt.

Vosmib (*taking it*) Ah, now, without my glasses I'm not very . . . and with them I'm even worse. My son can read it. Read it for me, will you, son. (*He gives the receipt to Pyotr.*)

Pyotr (*reading*) For the sale by me to Ivan Petrovich Vosmibratov, merchant of Kalinovsk . . .

Vosmib That's me, ma'am, that's me.

Pyotr (*reading*) . . . of my forest plot Scorched Acres and for nine acres of the Blazing Hill plot . . .

Vosmib Those are they . . .

Pyotr (*reading*) . . . I have received the payment in full, signed Raisa Gurmyzhskaya, Landowner.

Vosmib (*taking the receipt*) Beautiful. (*He takes out his wallet and carefully places the receipt inside it.*) Right. Here we go, then. (*He takes out money and starts to count it.*) One thousand . . . one thousand and three, five, seven . . . (*He hesitates, as if remembering.*) . . . eight. There we are, ma'am.

He hands the money to Gurmyzhskaya.

Gurmyz One thousand, eight hundred? But I need . . .

Vosmib Oh! Beg your pardon, ma'am, forgive me! What a memory, eh! (*He takes out his money again and hands over a further sum.*) There we are. Another two hundred roubles! That should make it right, shouldn't it? Yes? Pyotr? Pyotr! Come on speak up, lumber brain.

Pyotr That's right, sir!

Gurmyz Ivan Petrovich, you're joking, surely? You must be. It's three thousand, not two thousand.

Vosmib Three thousand? What you talking about, three?

Gurmyz You surely haven't forgotten? For the original plot, one and a half thousand and then a further one and a half thousand for the other plot.

Vosmib Oh no, that can't be right, ma'am. Not according to my calculations . . .

Gurmyz Your calculations?

Vosmib I'd hardly buy that amount of forest for three thousand, would I? Where would be the profit in that? I'd be cutting my own throat . . . That can't be right.

Gurmyz Of course it's right. Are you calling me a liar? Listen, I trusted you. I told everyone what a trustworthy man you were. What a good family man . . .

Vosmib With respect, that's totally beside the point, ma'am.

Gurmyz Well, if you're going to behave like this, then I'm afraid our agreement is null and void.

Vosmib Just as you like, ma'am. In that case, I bid you good day. Let's go, son!

Gurmyz No, come back! I'm sorry, I am not prepared to sell Scorched Acres and Blazing Hill for that sum, I'm sorry . . .

Vosmib Well, I'm sorry as well. If you've changed your mind about selling, you'd better give me the money back, hadn't you?

Gurmyz I'll tell you what I'll do, I'll keep one and a half thousand for Scorched Acres and you can have your five hundred back.

Vosmib Oh, dear. I think we need to do a bit of haggling here, don't we? Listen, I can't take less than two thousand for Blazing Hill. And even then, I'd be doing you a favour.

Gurmyz What are you talking about? Are you refusing to take this money back?

Vosmib I'm afraid I am, ma'am. You see, since I bought it off you, I can sell it on for what I like, you follow? And two thousand's the asking price.

Gurmyz But if I give you this two thousand back, I'll have given you Scorched Acres for nothing.

Vosmib I'm very much afraid that's your problem now, ma'am.

Gurmyz (*slightly hysterical*) I refuse to go through with this! Do you hear me? I refuse to go through with it . . . Please!

Vosmib Ah, there we are, you see! You look down your nose at us, don't you? But when the going gets rough . . .

Pyotr Dad!

Vosmib Shut up!

Gurmyz Please. I insist you take back this five hundred . . .

Vosmib Sorry, there's no point in arguing. I can't do it. Come on, son, let's go.

Gurmyz How can you behave like this?

Vosmib Listen, even a small child could understand it. I bought the forest off you, I gave you the money for it, you gave me a receipt for it; that means the forest belongs to me, and the money belongs to you. That's the end of it. I bid you a very good day.

Vosmibratov leaves followed by Pyotr.

Gurmyz It's daylight robbery! That's all it is. Why is it that whenever I buy or sell something, people always swindle me. I'm obviously a born victim. (*She goes on to the terrace. Calling*) Aleksis, please! Help me! Aleksis!

Neschastlivtsev and Bulanov appear.

Bulanov He has just been showing me the most amazing card tricks, you have no idea . . .

Gurmyz Aleksis, you won't believe it. I sold Ivan Petrovich part of the forest for three thousand and he refuses to pay me more than two . . .

Neschast What? Refuses, did you say? The miserable, cheating swine!

Gurmyz Well, there's nothing we can do about it now, I suppose. At least he gave me two.

Neschast (*angrily*) What do you mean, nothing? Fetch him back here! Call him back! I'll soon deal with him!

Gurmyz But he's got a receipt.

Neschast Who cares! I don't give a damn about receipts! Arkashka! Bring him here! I'll soon settle his hash! (*roaring*) Bring him here!

Enter Karp and Schastlivtsev.

Gurmyz (*to Bulanov*) Oh, isn't he terrifying! Let's go, let's go!

Bulanov I'd like to stay if I may, ma'am. I'm curious to see what happens.

Exit Gurmyzhskaya.

Has Ivan Petrovich left?

Karp Not yet. He's still here in the yard, sir.

Neschast Well, bring the scoundrel back here! If needs be, drag him in by his collar.

Exit Karp.

Arkashka, bring me my medals!

Schast Medals? Oh, right. Yes, your medals.

Exit Schastlivtsev.

Bulanov What are you going to say to him?

Neschast Haven't the faintest idea.

Bulanov But surely if he has documentary proof of sale there's nothing you can do, is there, sir?

Neschast There was never a document that could stop me, I tell you. I'm not a piddling little pen-pusher. Look, leave me alone would you, old chap, I need to get into – I need to muster my thoughts.

Schastlivtsev brings on a selection of prop medals. Neschastlivtsev puts them on.

Bulanov What medals are these, sir? Foreign ones?

Enter Karp, Vosmibratov and Pyotr.

Vosmib What's all this about? I got business to attend to. I can't waste time round here, talking.

Karp Please! He insists.

Bulanov Are they foreign medals, sir?

Neschast Yes, they're foreign. Now, buzz off! (*to Vosmibratov*) Come here.

Vosmib I should like to welcome you, squire. I don't know your name but –

Neschast Do as you're told and come here!

Vosmib Move that way a little, son.

He motions Pyotr to stand between him and Neschastlivtsev.

That's it, that'll do. (*to Neschastlivtsev*) What can I do for you, sir?

Neschast I can't talk to you when you're sixty feet away.

Vosmib That's quite alright with me, sir, you've got a good strong voice.

Neschast How dare you treat such a woman in that way . . .

Vosmib Beg pardon. What woman?

Neschast What woman! You have the gall to ask me what woman?

Vosmib I've no idea what you're –

Neschast
O woman! lovely woman! Nature made thee
To temper man: we had been brutes without you;
Angels are painted fair, to look like you . . .

Vosmib What's this all about?

Neschast Don't interrupt me! Just give thanks to God that I still have a gram of patience! (*with a gesture*) *O villain, villain, smiling, damned villain!*

Vosmib (*to Pyotr*) Don't just stand there gawping! Protect me!

Neschast (*roaring*) Callow youth! *Come not between the dragon and his wrath!*

Vosmib Listen, what are you shouting about? You keep shouting, I'll start shouting, alright?

Neschast You? You?

Vosmib Won't do either of us a blind bit of good . . .

Neschast You would shout at me?

Vosmib (*excitedly raising his voice*) Yes, I would. I can shout, too. If you keep shouting, I'll start shouting. I mean, two can shout, squire. If you're deaf or something, I don't mind shouting . . .

Neschast (*to Bulanov*) What's he saying? What's he saying? What's he daring to say? Haven't I killed him yet? What's he doing here?

Vosmib Listen, would somebody mind telling me what's going on? Tell me what you want 'cause I'm leaving in a minute.

Neschast What I want? He wants to know what I want! (*He laughs.*) Simply, I want to tell you you're a cheap swindler.

Vosmib Now that's out of order, squire. You stop that. There's no call for that!

Pyotr Charming, I'm sure.

Vosmib Come on, son.

Pyotr Yes, Dad.

Vosmib (*to Neschastlivtsev*) I'll come back when you have something to say to me that's civil. Let's go, son!

Neschast It doesn't bother you, I take it, that you've just swindled an honest woman?

Vosmib Swindled her? What are you talking about?

Neschast Are you calling her a liar as well?

Vosmib Did she tell you that?

Neschast You deny it?

Vosmib I most certainly do. Anyway, why believe her, not me?

Neschast He has the temerity to ask.

An angel! or, if not,
An earthly paragon!

Vosmib Look, don't start all that again! All I'm saying is . . . She's a little lacking in – financial acumen. If you get my meaning. I mean, what we're talking about here is just . . . standard business practice, isn't it?

Neschast Standard business practice? To hell with your business practice! Business practice is an insignificant speck of sand in the vast desert of existence. Whereas honesty – honesty is infinite. And honesty is something, my friend, you do not possess.

Vosmib Hey, hey, hey. No, I'm sorry, squire. Say what you like, but don't you start besmirking my honesty or I'll have you in court. What right have you to say I'm dishonest? I have documents here vindicating me. You ask anyone in the district about me, they'll say the same. Honest! And if that's not enough for you, you can hear the truth from my own mouth. I am an honest man. I don't brag about much, I'm not a bragger, squire, but as regards honesty you will not fault me there. I'll tell you this, and this is not an idle boast, as regards honesty, I am the benchmark, mate. Alright?

Neschast (*sitting, wearily*) Oh, go away!

Vosmib What do you mean, go away?

Neschast I've heard enough! Get out! *Oh, goodness how sad is our Russia!*

Vosmib Here, no, I'm not having this. Just a minute. Listen, one word, that's all it takes, one word from me and you are disabused, alright?

Neschast I am?

Vosmib You are. (*throwing his wallet on the table*) There.

Neschast What's this?

Vosmib Maybe your aunt's got a faulty memory, I'll give her the benefit of the doubt but if you prefer to believe her rather than me then good luck to her, on your conscience be it. Go on, take as much as you like. I won't stop you, help yourself.

Bulanov Quickly, take it!

Neschast (*to Bulanov*) Shut up! (*handing Vosmibratov back his wallet*) Give it to her yourself!

Vosmib Fair enough. (*counting out the money*) I want you all to witness this. When you say your prayers at night, include me.

Neschast The honourable thing. Your hand, sir!

Vosmib Eh? Well, yes, alright. (*Proffers his hand.*) Should have done this in the first place, shouldn't we? I tell you, squire, you certainly got the measure of me. That's the sort of man I am. When I get annoyed, in a temper, like, you know – well, nature will out – I give everything away, then. There you are, one thousand roubles. Can't do fairer than that.

Enter Gurmyzhskaya, who can't have been far away.

Ah, ma'am! (*handing her the money*) Here you are, ma'am.

Gurmyz Oh.

Vosmib If it hadn't been for this gentleman, you'd never have seen that money. But I'm a man of conscience. I wouldn't want it thought I was in the wrong. Not by anyone.

Gurmyz No, well, don't you be too cross with me, Ivan Petrovich, will you? I'm a woman, you see, you mustn't judge me too severely. Perhaps you'd like to come and have lunch with me tomorrow.

Vosmib Never say no to a spot of bread and salt. Besides we still have the timber concession to discuss, don't we?

Gurmyz Oh, yes, the timber . . .

Vosmib Sorry about all that. Good-bye, Colonel Lionsides, sir! Let's go, son.

Vosmibratov exits followed by Pyotr and Karp.

Gurmyz (*to Neschastlivtsev*) You don't know how grateful I am to you! And do you know, I've just remembered, what a coincidence, I owe you exactly this sum of money. An old debt of your father's that was repaid.

Neschast (*studiedly casual*) Really? Well. Any time, you know . . .

Gurmyzhskaya opens her box somewhat hurriedly, puts in the money and locks it again.

Gurmyz Just as you wish. I'll look after it in the meantime, I promise, my dear.

Neschast Aha! Auntie, if I didn't know you better I'd suspect you were trying to offer me money as delicately as possible, weren't you? Well, alright, I'll play along with it. You owe me, do you? Splendid. And I promise you, the minute I need it, I'll come and claim it, alright? At the moment I'm delighted to say, I don't need any, I'm flush.

Gurmyz Good.

Schast (*to himself*) What's he playing at, he's got less than I have?

Gurmyz (*glancing at Bulanov*) I hope you'll be stopping with us for a while.

Neschast Two, three days if I may, no more.

Gurmyz Why so few?

Neschast That's enough for me. To visit one's native woodlands, remembering days of foolish childhood, carefree youth . . .

Gurmyz Don't hurry away on my account. We adore having you here.

Neschast Dear lady! I'd love to stay. Believe me, my path ahead is thorny, but I shall not shrink from it.

Gurmyz (*indicating to Bulanov that she is very pleased*) As you wish, my dear. I just thought it might be more restful here.

Neschast My rest I will find in my grave. This is a paradise of which I am unworthy. But thank you, thank you! . . . *but sweeter yet, the still small voice of gratitude.* (*wiping away his tears*) But enough of that. Forgive me. I'm in danger of becoming a sentimental sycophant. I shall pray for you, Auntie!

He covers his face with his hand and exits. Schastlivtsev follows, but stops and watches from behind a bush.

Gurmyz I thought he'd never go. Well, I'm relieved he's not come here to cause any trouble. He's very – volatile, isn't he? Actually, I think underneath all that, he's rather dim. He was quite alarming with Vosmibratov, just now.

Bulanov Best way to deal with people like that, ma'am.

Gurmyz Nonetheless, be very careful, my dear. I still can't get that dream out of my head . . . he's potentially a violent man.

Bulanov Don't worry, we've become good friends, he and I. He's promised to teach me to play cards.

69

Gurmyz Really? I must say I was quite surprised . . . his refusing money. That was rather an attractive side of him. Mind you, I must have been out of my mind, mentioning that debt. I get so carried away sometimes I actually believe what I'm saying. I do so loathe parting with money unless it's absolutely unavoidable.

Bulanov You know the old saying, ma'am. Tight fist, open heart.

Gurmyz I'm not mean, you understand. I'll give everything I have to the man I fall in love with.

Bulanov I expect – that would be quite a lot, ma'am.

Gurmyz See for yourself! (*She opens the box.*) All that is for the one I love.

Bulanov (*looking inside, half to himself*) Grief!

Gurmyz Now, listen to me, Aleksis! I need to give you a little talking to. You're still far too servile. Most of the time you behave like a schoolboy. We must help you to become more mature, more assured. I want you to be substantial, Aleksis. You must go into town and order yourself a much better suit, something more *ample*. And buy yourself an expensive gold watch and a chain and – so on . . . And you ought to have plenty of money in your pocket. It'll give you more – aplomb.

She takes out of the box the money that Vosmibratov gave her.

There! This is a windfall. I got it by chance. Here, take it as a gift.

Bulanov (*flustered*) For me, ma'am? (*taking the money*) Thank you, ma'am! (*kissing her hand*) You want me to be more substantial? Then I shall be, I promise.

Gurmyz Good. Now, let's go and make a list of what to buy in town, shall we?

Exeunt.

Schast Good-bye, money! Oh, these tragedians!

If it's true the tragedian's art is far higher,
Than that to which humble comedians aspire,
That the tragic achievement is quite so immense,
Then how come that none of them has any sense?

Exits.

Act Four

*Another part of the garden. On the right the summer
house, to the left a garden bench. In the distance,
through the trees, a lake is visible. A moonlit night.
Neschastlivtsev and Schastlivtsev enter.*

Neschast Did you get any supper, old chap?

Schast I did.

Neschast Did they feed you well?

Schast Excellently. But then a clever man can survive
anywhere, you know.

Neschast A clever man? Who on earth can you be
talking about?

Schast Me, sir.

Neschast Has someone been telling you you're clever?
Well, don't you believe a word of it. They were having
you on.

Schast Extremely clever, in fact. First of all, I ate from
the mistress's menu. I told them that was what I was
used to. Secondly, I've become extremely friendly with
the housekeeper. Consequently I've not only managed to
borrow money off her but I've also got a bottle of cherry
brandy by my bed disguised as boot polish.

Neschast Not bad for a first performance, Arkashka, not
bad at all. Keep at it.

Schast I will. May I ask you something . . .

Neschast What?

Schast All that money. When he gave it to you. Put it into your hands. Why on earth did you give it back?

Neschast Have you gone mad, Arkashka? I gave it back because it wasn't mine.

Schast What's that got to do with it? Who cares? We could have been away from here, into town, rented a troika, caught the steamer to Yaroslavl, and then on to the fair at Nizhniy!

Neschast I think the solution is to strangle you, Arkashka. It would be better for you, and quieter for me.

Schast Go on, strangle me, if you like. The fact is, you may think you're clever but that grammar school boy is far cleverer. He was taking over your role just now.

Neschast Him? He's only a boy. What role?

Schast Leading man and lover.

Neschast Lover? (*threateningly*) Whose lover?

Schast Your aunt's.

Neschast You not only have a servant's mentality, Arkashka, you have a menial soul. Just be careful or someone will give you a good hiding.

Schast Won't be the first time . . .

Neschast (*moving towards him*) A damn good hiding.

Schast I don't care! (*moving away*) What's more she's given him that money instead and meanwhile you've been recast . . . (*from the bush*) . . . as the village idiot.

Neschast (*advancing on him*) Village idiot?

Schast (*retreating*) The local laughing stock.

73

Neschast (*advancing*) Laughing? At me? Who's laughing at me? Who?

Schast (*still retreating*) I'm not scared of you. I've done nothing wrong. I heard it with my own ears.

Neschast But who's been laughing at me?

Schast Your aunt and Bulanov.

Neschast (*clutching his head*) At me!

Schast Thought you were a fool. Rather dim, she said.

Neschast Arkashka! Are you tired of life or what? Why don't you just go and hang yourself?

Schast You had the money in your hands and you let it flow through your fingers like pond water. And you wanted me as a partner! Alright, if I'm supposed to be your partner, then it's fifty–fifty. In which case, you know what you did? You gave away my half as well as yours, that's what you did.

Neschast I didn't invite you to be a partner in crime, for God's sake.

Schast Give me my half. I want my half.

Neschast Arkashka! Are you drunk?

Schast Yes, I am. I'm drunk and proud of it.

Neschast No, I'm sorry. You're going to have to die. I'm going to have to kill you.

Schast (*retreating*) You can't kill me, your arms are too short!

Neschast You're lying! Please say you're lying! My aunt? My dearest aunt, that embodiment of kindness and humility . . . laughing at me? No! I shall have to speak

74

to her, get to the truth. No. That I could never forgive!
Never. Village idiot?

He goes off.
  Schastlivtsev sits on the bench.

Schast (*to himself*) A thousand roubles! Tragedians.
Shoot them, I say.

  Ulita enters and looks around.

Hallo. Taking a stroll?

Ulita Yes. The night is so . . . Isn't it?

Schast Yes . . .

Ulita I love just looking up at the . . .

Schast Yes . . . yes . . .

Ulita So beautiful.

  Pause.

Have you tried the cherry brandy yet? I didn't know if it
was any good. I hope it is.

Schast It's very good, excellent. So good I thought you
must have made it yourself.

Ulita No, I – Oh, you're laughing at me again, aren't
you?

  Karp enters. He stops as he sees them both.

Schast Ah! Swordfish. Good evening.

  Karp gives him a look.

Ulita You visiting us for long?

Schast Shouldn't think so. No much to do here, is there?

Karp Be a good thing if he did stay, your master. You see the way Ivan Petrovich handed back that money? Straight away.

Ulita Well, he would hand it back to a man, wouldn't he?

Karp My point exactly. I mean, the way things are going with the mistress . . . well! Sensible people buy things, she seems to spend all the time selling. Forest, timber . . .

Ulita (*aware of Schastlivtsev*) That's enough, now . . .

Karp And what does she do with the money? Crams it all in that box of hers. Hanging on to it all for grim death one minute, the next she's throwing it about – money flying everywhere . . .

Schast Really?

Karp The air's full of it . . .

Ulita She only gives it to the poor or to relatives . . .

Schast Wonder how you go about catching some?

Karp There's some as manage to do it.

Ulita . . . to the poor and her relatives, that's all . . .

Karp They'd be lucky.

Ulita Who else, then?

Karp Want me to list them for you? The French doctor, the Italian landscape gardener, the Portuguese –

Ulita You ought to be ashamed of yourself. In front of a stranger, too.

Karp Come on, he's one of us, isn't he?

Ulita All the same, you shouldn't criticise the mistress.

Karp I'm not criticising, I'm just saying. That's all. Just saying.

Schast Interesting conversation.

Ulita Nothing interesting about it. He's making it all up.

Karp It's the truth. I'm off to bed. 'Night.

Schast Goodnight. Sleep well, old sturgeon.

Karp (*scowling*) Stupid valet.

He goes.

Ulita Pay no attention to him.

Schast No?

Ulita Would you like me to bring you some cream for your tea tomorrow?

Schast Only if it's from an angry bull.

Ulita What? Honestly! I don't know what you're talking about.

Schast I mean rum. That's what we call it. Angry bull's milk.

Ulita I'll have a look.

Schast Please. If you love me . . .

Ulita You're just making fun of me again, aren't you? You mustn't laugh at us women . . .

Schast Laugh at them? I take women extremely seriously . . .

Ulita Men can afford to make jokes. They have no real responsibilities. But you just put yourself in our place! Imagine what life's been like for someone like me. Life? You could hardly call it living. Existing, more like.

77

Barely that, really. We weren't allowed to get married, not even allowed to fall in love with anyone . . . Love was completely banned. Your only hope of a future was to keep in sweet with your mistress. Grovelling, crawling, worse than an animal. Then if you were good, you earned yourself little privileges. Put some hope back in your heart. Because the feeling's still alive in there, isn't it? It's still crying out inside you, begging to be – Oh, I tell you, this serfdom makes you feel so ugly, so unwanted. I'd give you my whole life story . . . only you'd be bored to death . . . quite rightly. Why shouldn't you? A mean little story with no laughs in it at all. Why upset someone I like. Or myself, neither. (*Pause.*) Just now, I couldn't help overhearing . . .

Schast What?

Ulita Your master shouting at you.

Schast Oh, that . . .

Ulita Threatening to kill you. He always looks so fierce. Terrifying. Frightens the life out of me.

Schast He's an idiot.

Ulita How can you stay with a master like that?

Schast Master? I'm every bit as good as he is. All he does is shout about the place and put on airs.

Ulita Yes, maybe. But he's still of noble birth, isn't he? You can't deny him that, can you?

Schast I'm not denying him anything! All I'm saying is that he and I are equals. The only difference between us is that he plays tragedies and I play comedies. We're both actors and we're both drunks.

Ulita Actors? What are you saying?

78

Schast We've been wandering all over Russia from theatre to theatre for more than ten years now, like gypsies. That's why he hasn't been to see his aunt. He was ashamed to show his face.

Ulita How awful!

Schast He was on his way to Vologda on foot with his little bag. He couldn't show himself here without a servant, could he? After all, he is a nobleman. He dragged me in on the act. He's not even a good actor. I'm better than him. Old barnstorming ham. His style went out years ago.

Ulita I can't believe what you're telling me.

Schast He's hoping to get something out of his aunt, that's all. He couldn't plead poverty straightaway, that would be too big a blow to his pride. I tell you, he's a very violent, dangerous, unstable character. He'll kill somebody one of these days, mark my words.

Ulita (*in alarm*) It's a good job you told me! Terrifying! I'm going indoors at once.

Schast Going? Don't go.

Ulita You're an actor as well, you say?

Schast I am.

Ulita Then I'm not staying out here. It's not safe.

Schast No, you may be right. Particularly since I specialise, you see . . .

Ulita Specialise?

Schast In playing the devil! And I'll tell you this. I won't rest until I see the lot of you in hell!

He gives a blood-curdling, maniacal laugh.

Ulita (*rushing away*) Oh, dear God!

Schast (*yelling after her*) To hell with your bloody country estate. To hell with the lot of you!

Ulita has gone.

Oh, well. That's blown the fuck. Celibate again. I've had enough of all this. I'm off. (*He hesitates.*) Except that bloody village is full of dogs. Typical stupid peasants. Nothing to eat themselves, so they breed sodding great dogs. Anyway, I'm not leaving my library behind. Or the rest of my cherry brandy. He's bound to be still awake, though. If I go in now, he'll give me a quick soliloquy from *Lear* and I'll finish up flying through the window again. I'll go for a walk in the garden for a bit. Probably trample all her dahlias but never mind.

Schastlivtsev exits. Pyotr creeps cautiously out of the shadows.

Pyotr I thought he'd never go to bed. I don't trust him. He looks as if he'd sell his own father for half a rouble. (*looking up at the house*) Come on, Aksyusha! Maybe she won't come. Oh, but I have to see her! Even if it's only for the last time. I can't stop shaking. It's easier to go thieving! Is this what love does to you? Dad says it doesn't last. Couple of years it'll wear off, he says. Then you can get back to the serious business of making money. In the meantime, lie back and enjoy the misery. Is that her? Yes. She's coming.

Enter Aksyusha. She runs to Pyotr.

Aksyusha Oh, at last!

Pyotr I've been hanging around here for ages. (*Kisses her.*)

Aksyusha Quickly, we've very little time before they notice I'm missing. What happened?

Pyotr Well, I've had another talk with my dad.

Aksyusha And?

Pyotr He's giving in. He yelled at me for an hour or so as usual. Then he says, 'You're so thick you'll never find a bride with a decent dowry. If you can find one with two thousand, I'll settle for that, alright?'

Aksyusha But there's nowhere I can get two thousand any more than three!

Pyotr We've got to find it somehow.

Aksyusha I'd never get it from Raisa Pavlovna. Not if I crawled to her on my hands and knees.

Pyotr You could ask your cousin.

Aksyusha Oh, no, I couldn't!

Pyotr Appeal to him as family. He's family!

Aksyusha I'd have to tell him everything.

Pyotr So what! Tell him! He's our only hope.

Aksyusha Our last hope.

Pyotr Underneath all that, he seems a good bloke. He'll be on our side. Talk to him first thing tomorrow. Dad and I are coming over at midday. You can tell me then how it went.

Aksyusha Alright.

Pyotr Just be straight with him. Tell him it's . . . I don't know . . .

Aksyusha Life or death . . .

Pyotr What?

Aksyusha Nothing.

Pyotr Oh, come on. Don't talk like that.

Aksyusha That's how I feel, Petya! A sort of terrible emptiness.

Pyotr Why?

Aksyusha I can't tell you why. I think all the unhappiness, all the misery of my childhood – it's eaten away my heart. It's as if I'm frightened to feel any more. I'm all alone, you see, Petya. Other people have a mother, a grandmother, even a nanny or a friend. Someone they can talk to, share things with. I have no one. I can't even cry . . . I tell you, my heart's empty, Petya. Whilst my head's – my head's whirling with thoughts and thinking and thoughts.

Pyotr (*grasping her*) Stop thinking! It's nothing but trouble.

Aksyusha (*clinging to him*) Hold me, reassure me, talk to me . . . Petya, ever since we last talked, I find myself standing at the edge of the lake. I walk away but then I'm drawn back. It's as if –

Pyotr Water?

Aksyusha When I'm walking in the garden, I can't take my eyes off the lake. I deliberately walk further away from it, but it draws me back. I only have to glimpse it through the trees and it's as if some power has taken hold of me, dragging me towards it . . .

Pyotr Stop it, now!

Aksyusha I could! I could so easily throw myself in . . .

Pyotr Where's this coming from? It's wrong to think like this . . .

Aksyusha I don't know. What you said yesterday stayed

82

in my mind: 'Choose the steepest, deepest ravine, and find out whether we float or sink to the bottom.' I keep imagining sinking. All around me it's so green. Peaceful. It's not that I want to die. Yes, of course, life is still possible. We can carry on deceiving them for a while, even run away together for a time. When I got back they wouldn't kill me. They'd still have to carry on feeding me and clothing me, however badly. Life would go on . . .

Pyotr What sort of a life is that? That's how dogs live; people deserve better than that . . .

Aksyusha That's exactly what I'm saying. You *can* live like that, but is it worth it? Oh, I don't understand what's happened to me. I'm behaving like a sixteen-year-old – though at sixteen I was in control of my life . . . Oh, my sweet love, you can't believe how unhappy I am because of you. (*She embraces him.*)

Pyotr My poor darling! Where did you learn to love like this? Why does one touch from you tear my heart apart? No one else has done that to me. No one ever in the whole world. Only you! What do I have to do not to lose you?

Aksyusha I can't give you the answer to that.

Pyotr Look, let's not make hasty decisions. Let things stay as they are. At least till you've talked to your cousin. Let's see what he says first.

Aksyusha Alright.

Pyotr Who knows, he might be able to help us.

Aksyusha Maybe. It's time you went.

Pyotr You go back indoors, Aksyusha. And don't even think about . . . God protect you!

Aksyusha Go on! Don't worry about me. While there's still hope . . .

Pyotr There he is, your cousin, look! Now's your chance. (*They kiss.*) Yes, there's still hope. You're my hope.

> *Pyotr exits.*
> *Aksyusha turns as if to go into the house but Neschastlivtsev appears before she can.*

Neschast Great heavens! Behold, a beautiful woman!

> *Aksyusha freezes.*

(*approaching*) Are you a woman or a departed soul?

Aksyusha Cousin!

Neschast Ah, yes! I see, you're all too clearly flesh and blood. I'm afraid, on a beautiful night such as this, I'm safer communing with the dear departed.

Aksyusha Cousin!

Neschast I'm sorry, I'm too depressed at present to converse with the living. I'm looking for some kindred suffering spirit who has quit this mortal coil. Go away, girl!

Aksyusha Cousin, I too have suffered and I'm still suffering.

Neschast You?

Aksyusha I'm terribly unhappy.

Neschast (*beckoning her to him*) Then come here at once.

> *Aksyusha leans on his chest.*

84

We are cousins twice over, then: cousins by blood and cousins in unhappiness.

Aksyusha (*falling on her knees*) Oh, cousin, I'm guilty ...

Neschast (*raising her up*) What's that you're saying? Guilty? What, you? So young, so beautiful? Compared to whom? Me? Humanity's refuse tip?

Aksyusha I'm guilty. You see, I love ...

Neschast Love? My dear child! That's why God gave you a heart, to love.

Aksyusha You don't understand. I'm in love. I'm sick with love. I must marry him, I must, I must!

Neschast And who's stopping you?

Aksyusha People. People with power over us.

Neschast Don't you listen to them! Marry the one you love. You have my blessing!

Aksyusha He can't marry me without a dowry, his father won't let him. I need a dowry, but I don't have one.

Neschast Poppycock! Happiness is worth more than money.

Aksyusha I can have no happiness without money.

Neschast How much do you need?

Aksyusha Two thousand roubles.

Neschast A mere bagatelle! Surely Raisa Pavlovna won't refuse such a small sum?

Aksyusha She will. She already keeps me, feeds me out of charity. That's quite enough as far as she's concerned.

Neschast And you're telling me that your future happiness depends on such a piddling sum . . .?

Aksyusha Not just my happiness, my life.

Neschast Your life? Your *life*? Great heavens above! Is that true?

Aksyusha Yes, cousin. If we can't be together, I shall die.

Neschast At last, dear God, at last ! O *tiger's heart wrapp'd in a woman's hide!* Your love is truly more than a passing fancy? You're really prepared to sacrifice everything?

Aksyusha I've given so much for my love. Why not my life?

Neschast You're not afraid?

Aksyusha No. Though I was hoping there might be a chance, cousin –

Neschast (*lifting his arms above his head*) *Angels and ministers of grace defend thee*!

He envelops her in his arms. A short pause.

Aksyusha Cousin, you mustn't be angry with me, you mustn't think badly of me . . . This is hard for me to say . . .

Neschast Speak, child, speak!

Aksyusha I don't want you to think I'm a scheming, begging relative. Please don't think that! My mother and I were very poor but never once, all through my childhood, did I ask for anything from anyone. I worked. But now, cousin, I'm reduced to begging. I'm begging you. Thank goodness it's dark and you can't see how ashamed I am. Cousin, you're rich, you're single. Give me my happiness, give me my life. (*She drops to her knees.*)

Neschast (*lifting her up, moved*) My child! My dear child!

Aksyusha Will you be the father I never had?

Neschast Oh, my poor child! I have to tell you, I'm a total fraud. A criminal. Yes, I could have had money, I could have helped you, I could have made you happy, but, you see, I've squandered it, frittered it away; chucked it in the dirt together with my own youth. With my entire life. And now when it's genuinely needed, I don't have any. If only I'd known! If I'd known, if every time I laid my hands on a rouble, I hadn't . . . Dear God, look at me! Drinking, shouting, swearing, ranting, bragging of my pathetic sexual conquests, reeking of cherry brandy. And here's my poor little cousin, trembling between life and death. Weep, you drunken bastard, weep!

Aksyusha (*somewhat alarmed*) Cousin, cousin!

Neschast Forgive me, forgive me! The fact is, my dear, I'm poorer than you are, you see. I arrived here on foot. I walked five hundred miles to see my relatives. I'm wearing my one decent suit so I wouldn't get chucked out. I'm flattered you think I'm even good for two thousand. I'm not. I'm good for nothing. Cousin, you shouldn't be asking me for money. It's the wrong way round entirely. I tell you what, the next time someone bangs on your window begging for five kopecks for a hair of the dog, don't say no to him because that'll be me.

Aksyusha (*clutching her heart*) You mean I've humiliated myself for nothing. What a stupid fool I am. I'd hoped . . . for a moment I really hoped . . . what right has someone like me to hope . . . goodbye . . .

She walks away, unsteadily at first, then faster until she finally breaks into a run.

Neschast (*looking after her*) No! No! Cousin, you're too young to die!

He runs off after her.
Enter Schastlivtsev.

Schast Where's he off to? Gone to drown himself hopefully. Best place for him! I can nip into the summer house and collect my library. I'll hide in the bushes till it's light, then I'm away! At least I've managed to borrow some money. My luck must be changing. Usually people aren't that trusting. All I've got to do then is find a theatre company that hasn't gone bankrupt.

He goes into the summer house.
Neschastlivtsev enters, supporting Aksyusha, who is wet and barely able to walk.

Neschast No, I'm sorry, my child, I don't care how unhappy you are, I refuse to let you drown. For heaven's sake, you haven't even lived properly yet. You're young! You can't be so unhappy you're tired of life already, surely? Forget the past, leave that behind you! We'll start a new life, child, and dedicate it to the glory of art! What do you say to that?

Aksyusha What? I don't know. I don't know anything any more. I want to die. Let me rest.

Neschast (*sitting her down on the bench*) What are you saying? You don't know anything? Well, that's just not true, my child. You already know more than most. You know inner turmoil, you know passion – that's enough!

Aksyusha Do what you want with me. I've nothing to live for now. Whatever life you're suggesting . . . it can't be worse than this.

Neschast Make no mistake, there's sorrow where we're going, my child. But, to balance that, there's a joy which ordinary people can never experience. Look at it this way. Why should you wear out your precious soul for nothing! These priceless emotions of yours, these pearls of passion, these diamond tears? Who's here to appreciate them apart from me? Not a soul. But where we're going . . . Oh! If you cast even half these emotional jewels before an audience, you'll have them applauding in the aisles. You'll be showered with flowers, gifts . . . not a dry eye in the house. Look at me. I'm a beggar, a pathetic down-and-out. But on stage I'm a prince. I become the prince. I live his life, I'm tormented by his thoughts, I cry his tears over poor Ophelia and I love her in a way that forty thousand suitors couldn't love her. And you! You're young, beautiful, you have fire in your eyes, music in your speech, beauty in every movement. You'll appear on the stage a queen and you'll come off the stage a queen, and that's how they'll remember you for ever.

Aksyusha I'm dead, cousin, dead.

Neschast We'll bring you back to life, I promise. The first sounds of the overture will do that. Overture and beginners, please!

Aksyusha And Petya? What about Petya?

Neschast Cousin, you're a woman and I promise you, women soon forget. You'll forget him like any other first love. There'll soon be hundreds of rich, handsome young men trying to catch your attention, hanging on your every word.

Aksyusha (*shaking her head*) I wouldn't want that.

Neschast No? Better still. Send them all packing with the contempt they deserve. Fall in love with a penniless artist instead. Much more worthwhile. It's your choice, my child! What do you say?

Aksyusha (*in a small voice*) Alright.

Neschast You'll be my pride and glory. And, yes, I will. I'll be like a father to you, I shall be your protector and nursemaid and . . . Come on! It'd be a sin to sleep on a night like this. I have several playscripts with me. I'd like to read a few of them to you. This night is dedicated to you, my dear, for tonight an actress is born!

Aksyusha Let's go!

> *They walk towards the summer house. As they do so, Schastlivtsev comes out with a bundle.*

Schast (*seeing them*) Oh, no . . .

Neschast Hold it there, you ship's rat! I'm in generous mood, I forgive you. We've something to celebrate, Arkashka! Meet our new actress. Together we shall travel round all the theatres, see the whole of Russia.

Schast (*as they go in, after them*) Did you drink my cherry . . .?

> *They go into the summer house.*
> *Gurmyzhskaya and Ulita enter.*

Gurmyz You spoke to him?

Ulita I did, mistress. I was circumspectual, though. The mistress, I said, she can't sleep, because the weather's unusual. She's walking about the garden, and she's probably lonely as she's on her own. And there's you, sir, I says, lying there enjoying yourself in bed. What sort of a gentleman does that make you? He jumped up like a shot, starts getting dressed.

Gurmyz Good, good.

Ulita There's something else as well, mistress, but I don't quite know how to tell you.

Gurmyz What's the matter?

Ulita The young lady's gone off somewhere.

Gurmyz Gone?

Ulita She's not in her room and her bed's not been slept in.

Gurmyz Well, that's wonderful.

Ulita How do you mean, mistress?

Gurmyz I'm delighted. I'm sick and tired of the girl, I've been looking for an excuse to get rid of her. This is perfect. With behaviour like that, she's certainly not worthy of him.

Ulita I'll say she's not! I always wondered what a fine handsome gentleman like him ever found to . . .

Gurmyz Well, that's none of your business.

Ulita No, ma'am. I've found something else out as well, but I'm a little frightened to tell you. I mean, when I heard, it shook me. Shook me to my roots . . .

Gurmyz How many times do I have to tell you not to talk like that? I have a nervous disposition. You know that perfectly well. You're always terrifying me to the point of hysteria and then telling me some trivial piece of nonsense. The fire's gone out. The roof's leaking . . .

Ulita Oh, this is far from trivial, mistress, don't worry. It's Gennadiy Dem'yanych.

Gurmyz What about him?

Ulita It seems he's been deceiving you. He's no gentleman. He's an actor. He calls himself Neschastlivtsev. He's also apparently a drunkard. All he has in the world are the clothes he stands up in. He arrived here on foot with a knapsack.

Gurmyz So, he's Neschastlivtsev, I've heard of him, I've heard of him. Well, that's even better.

Ulita His servant's an actor, too. He's even worse. He specialises in the devil.

Gurmyz I don't know what you're talking about but this is wonderful!

Ulita How do you mean, mistress?

Gurmyz Because by tomorrow morning they won't be here. Any of them. I'm not running an hotel for riff-raff.

Ulita Quite right, ma'am. Why should you? May I kiss your hand? (*She does so. Quietly*) Aleksey Sergeyevich is coming.

Ulita moves away.

Now here's a proper gentleman.

Ulita exits as Bulanov appears, still straightening his clothes.

Bulanov Why didn't you send for me sooner, Raisa Pavlovna? If only you'd told me, ma'am . . .

Gurmyz Told you what?

Bulanov That you liked going for walks at night, ma'am.

Gurmyz Why should you care? I love nature, you probably don't.

Bulanov I'm quite prepared to love it, ma'am. If you're lonely, you have only to –

Gurmyz Don't you feel lonely, too, on such a night? Aren't you affected by the moon, the air, this feeling of freshness? Look, how the lake glistens, the shadows that are cast by the trees! Are you indifferent to all that?

Bulanov No, ma'am, what do you mean indifferent! (*waving vaguely*) Stars. It's just I don't know what to do for the best to please you, ma'am. I only want to know what gives you pleasure.

Gurmyz Well, what do you think gives me pleasure? I'd be interested to hear. What do you think pleases me? Come on.

Bulanov (*hesitating*) The moon, ma'am?

Gurmyz Oh, sweet simple boy! Yes, once upon a time I used to adore the moon, but I grew out of that a long time ago. I'm not sixteen any more.

Bulanov (*thinking*) Your relatives then, ma'am?

Gurmyz My relatives! (*laughing*) Relatives! Dear God, do you want me to die laughing? You're adorably naive. (*laughing again*) Relatives!

Bulanov I'm sorry, ma'am.

Gurmyz Come on, come on. More things to please me. Come on.

Bulanov I don't know any more, ma'am!

Gurmyz (*moving closer to him*) Then you're a fool, aren't you? You're a fool.

Bulanov Yes, ma'am . . . I did think perhaps . . . but only to myself . . . I didn't dare . . . If only you'd said something before . . . I mean, I've been here some time, ma'am . . . This is what I've dreamt of, my sweet Raisa! You should have said something before . . .

He embraces Gurmyzhskaya and tries to kiss her.

Gurmyz (*pushing him away*) What do you think you're doing? Are you out of your mind? Take your hands off me, you ill-bred little boy!

Gurmyzhskaya exits.

Bulanov What have I done? You fool! (*shouting after Gurmyzhskaya*) I'm sorry, ma'am! (*to himself*) Tomorrow she'll throw me out on my ear! (*shouting louder*) I'm sorry!

Collapses on the bench.

I've done it now. I'm ruined. I've ruined everything!

Act Five

Scene as Act One.
  Karp is clearing up the cups from the table. He sees Gurmyzhskaya's box.

Karp That's odd. She'll be looking for that later. Better not touch the treasury. Leave it where it is.

  Enter Bulanov.

Bulanov Karp, where on earth's the tea?

Karp Aren't we waiting for Gennadiy Dem'yanych?

Bulanov Certainly not.

Karp Just as you like.

Bulanov And when he does turn up, you're to let me know, but on no account disturb Raisa Pavlovna!

Karp Right you are.

Bulanov And, Karp, in future I expect you to carry out my orders promptly and without question. I will not stand for disobedience. You're not dealing with Raisa Pavlovna. I shall expect you at my beck and call, or out you'll go, all of you. Alright? I shan't miss a trick.

Karp (*muttering*) What's got into you this morning.

Bulanov And no muttering. I don't like it.

Karp (*sotto*) Alright to breathe?

Bulanov Go on, get out . . .

  Exit Karp.

(*pleased with himself*) Hmm!

Enter Neschastlivtsev.

Neschast Good day.

Bulanov Good day to you, Mr Neschastlivtsev!

Neschast Ah. You know, do you?

Bulanov I do.

Neschast Well, I'm very glad to hear it, old chap. Now you know who you're dealing with, you'd better show a bit of respect, hadn't you?

Bulanov Respect? What, for an obscure provincial actor?

Neschast I think I'm going to have to teach you some manners, you know.

Bulanov If you're physically threatening me, I'd be very careful at your age.

Neschast Thanks for the tip. What do you suggest instead? Firearms? No, I think I still fancy my chances with my fists . . . (*He advances.*)

Bulanov (*stepping back*) Listen, let's stop all this, shall we? Just tell me who you've come to see?

Neschast Not you, certainly.

Bulanov Who then?

Neschast Listen, pin brain, this is my family home. I've come to drink tea with Auntie. So why don't you collect your satchel, get someone to wipe your ass for you and then piss off back to nursery school.

Bulanov Excuse me . . .

Neschast I do. Bye bye, off you go.

Bulanov When you've quite finished. Raisa Pavlovna apologises but she can't receive you. She's feeling unwell and, consequently, visits – even from family – would tire her at present.

Neschast I see. She's driving me out, is she? (*Pause.*) Do you know why?

Bulanov It's nothing to do with me. I think she just finds your presence here – disruptive. I'll say no more than that.

Neschast Very well! If that's her attitude! It doesn't matter that I loved her. Considered her as a second mother. (*Wipes away a tear.*) What's wrong with being an actor? We all do what we do best. At least I'm not a thief. I earn my bread by hard, honest labour. I didn't come here to beg for charity. Just for a spot of human warmth and kindness. I want you to know I am deeply hurt. And why does she send you to tell me, of all people? You . . .

Bulanov Now there is no need to –

Neschast Oh, God! He's starting to talk again! Listen, you mewling, puking schoolboy! Purely out of respect for this house I shan't beat the living daylight out of you. But if I ever meet up with you anywhere else, I'm warning you . . .

Bulanov Oh yes? We'll see about that.

Neschast Shut up, you ink-stained oik, you filthy, pee-smelling fourth former, you spotty little adolescent supporting juvenile . . .

Bulanov Will you please be quiet! You'll disturb Raisa Pavlovna. If you have a message for her, I'll pass it on.

Neschast Very well, excremental errand boy, you tell Raisa Pavlovna that it's not her I'm angry with, that

I should have liked to have said a proper goodbye to her but that if she doesn't want to, good luck to her.

Bulanov I'll tell her, sir.

Neschastlivtsev starts to leave. As he does so he notices the box.

Neschast (*to himself*) Hallo. Interesting.

Bulanov Anything else?

Neschast Nothing at all. Farewell, pubescent repugnance.

Neschastlivtsev goes off.
Gurmyzhskaya enters cautiously.

Gurmyz Bravo! Well, he certainly won't come back here again. (*Sits by the window.*) Yes, you do have a certain unexpected *je ne sais quoi*, I'm impressed.

Bulanov A lot, Raisa, depends on the circumstances. What have I been in this house up till now? Little more than a parasite. You must admit, it's very difficult for a dependant to retain any dignity.

Gurmyz I'm still cross with you about last night, though.

Bulanov Raisa, put yourself in my place! I was so overcome . . .

Gurmyz There's a way to go about these things, my dear. Imagine how I felt. Whatever possessed you? You must be aware of my reputation, surely? How could you . . .?

Bulanov (*kissing her hand*) Forgive me.

Gurmyz I do, my dear, I do forgive you. As a rule, I'm extremely broad-minded, I think that's my weakness. But you must always respect a woman's finer feelings.

Bulanov I know. I've a lot to learn. What can I say? But guided by your love and experience . . . If only I can get established here, just you watch. I'll reorganise the whole estate. And, Raisa, as far as I'm concerned, your interests will always come first, believe me . . .

Gurmyz I do believe you, my dear. Would you call Aksyusha for me?.

Bulanov Yes, we must think what to do about that girl.

Gurmyz There's no need to think about her at all! Especially not you, my dear! It's nothing to do with you. You must forget about her completely now. She slunk out of the house last night, we must send her packing.

Bulanov She was with Gennadiy Dem'yanych. He spent all night spouting soliloquies at her.

Gurmyz How do you know that? Look me in the eye.

Bulanov I saw them as I was passing the summer house.

Gurmyz I see. Nevertheless, she can't stay here.

Bulanov (*with a smile*) Starting to take precautions already, are you?

Gurmyz Necessary ones. You, my dear, are far too young to be entirely trusted.

Bulanov You can't just throw her out into the street, surely. She has no one. You'll have to marry her off.

Gurmyz Yes, but if I marry her off from this house, that makes things official and then she'll have to be given a dowry. And why on earth should I start wasting money on her? It would be an act of sheer lunacy.

Bulanov No, good point. You're quite right, no more unnecessary expenditure. Perhaps someone will take her without a dowry.

Gurmyz Well, that would be marvellous. That way we could observe all the *convenance* with a minimum of expense. Let's organise a party and we'll both give the couple our blessing. (*smiling at Bulanov rather coyly*) Their surrogate mother and father. (*seeing Aksyusha approaching*) Ah, here she is, she's coming. Go, my dear, go!

Bulanov leaves swiftly as Aksyusha enters.

Aksyusha You wanted to see me?

Gurmyz (*getting up*) Yes. Now, listen to me, Aksyusha. I don't want you to be under any illusion. You seem to think you can carry on living here for ever. Maybe I'm a little to blame, if you were under that impression. There was a time when I considered giving you in marriage to Aleksey Sergeyevich. But, from now on, you mustn't even think about him.

Aksyusha I never do.

Gurmyz No? Well, I don't believe you, but that's neither here nor there. You see, I soon realised that you two would not make a satisfactory match. Quite frankly you're unworthy of that man. It'd be ridiculous for you even to dream about him. (*Slight pause.*) Don't you want to say something?

Aksyusha I'm listening.

Gurmyz I'm afraid he's not for you, my dear. I hope you're not too disappointed. Tell me, did he make – overtures to you . . .?

Aksyusha Maybe.

Gurmyz Well, you must understand that they meant nothing. Sadly, you were just an object of idle male fancy. Possibly you flirted with him? Did you?

Aksyusha No.

Gurmyz I take it that means you did. Nonetheless, I have to tell you – and I hope this isn't going to hurt you too deeply – he doesn't like you. Indeed, I also have to break the news that he's in love with someone else.

Aksyusha What do I care?

Gurmyz You're not fooling me, my dear. Anyway, since he's no longer your fiancé, you can't possibly carry on living in the same house.

Aksyusha Just as you wish.

Gurmyz You're going to have to leave here, you understand?

Aksyusha Whenever you say.

Gurmyz Have you any idea where you'll go?

Aksyusha Thank you for your concern but once I leave this house you really don't have to bother about me any more.

Gurmyz I hope you're not thinking of settling down somewhere locally?

Aksyusha (*to herself*) The old girl's jealous.

Gurmyz What's that? I said, as long as you don't move to the town.

Aksyusha I might.

Gurmyz No, that would be impossible.

Aksyusha Why impossible, Raisa Pavlovna, you don't own the town, surely?

Gurmyz It's too near.

Aksyusha It's not far.

Gurmyz Aksyusha, my dear, don't you have any relatives further away? I'm happy to pay your expenses. If you must know, my darling, I'm worried for you. Let's face it, Aleksis can be thoughtless . . .

Aksyusha Yes, he's – completely lacking in thought . . .

Gurmyz You've noticed?

Aksyusha It's difficult not to. And, yes, if I'd wanted to, I've no doubt I could easily have . . .

Gurmyz Aha! There you are, you see. You admit it. Come here, my dear.

Gurmyzhskaya embraces Aksyusha.

You will move away, won't you? For me?

Aksyusha For you? Oh, now that's a little nearer the truth, isn't it? Why not admit it? You don't care at all what happens to me. You're simply jealous. A well-bred woman, jealous of a street urchin in case she steals her lover.

Gurmyz What are you talking about?

Aksyusha It's true. Why not be honest for once in your life? Instead of claiming to be a saint and making out the rest of us are sinners?

Gurmyz My dear, I'm also a woman . . .

Aksyusha Then come on, behave like a woman and admit that you're jealous! And I promise I'll move to the other end of the country and never bother you again.

Gurmyz You want me to reveal my weakness to you? (*embracing her*) Alright. Yes, I am jealous.

Aksyusha That's all I needed to hear. I'll go far, far away, don't worry.

She tries to kiss Gurmyzhskaya's hand.

Gurmyz What's that for, my dear?

Aksyusha For my board and lodging.

Gurmyz Oh, don't, don't! (*Kisses her.*) God grant you every happiness!

Aksyusha I'll pack my things.

Aksyusha goes out.

Gurmyz (*sits down by the window*) Well, I think that's everything settled, thank God. I can at last relax and enjoy myself. Oh, these appalling relatives! Aleksis can take care of the estate whilst I occupy myself with charitable work. I'll put aside a small sum for that. It needn't be very much . . .

Karp enters.

Karp Gennadiy Dem'yanych wishes to see you.

Gurmyz Oh, no! Tell him that I've –

Karp But he's here, ma'am, and he won't listen to reason.

Neschast (*off*) Auntie!

Gurmyz Oh, dear God! He's back again.

Neschastlivtsev enters wearing his travelling clothes. He takes off his knapsack and puts it in the corner, together with his stick.

Neschast Leave us, Karp, and don't let anyone in! Tell them we're busy.

Karp Yes, sir.

Karp exits.

Gurmyz What's that ghastly suit you're wearing?

Neschast It's my travelling suit. This suit is an old friend and companion. I've wandered in this suit through thunderstorms, like King Lear, seeking shelter. And I have been received in this suit, received by strangers with more warmth than by my own family. Farewell!

Gurmyz Good-bye, my dear.

Neschast Two more words and I will never trouble you again.

Gurmyz I'm listening. (*She picks up the handbell.*)

Neschast What are you doing? You going to ring the bell? Not yet. Give it here!

He takes the handbell from her.

I'll ring it when it's time. We don't need witnesses. On the contrary, Auntie, you make certain that no one comes in here, especially Bulanov, if his wretched life means anything to you at all.

Gurmyz (*humouring him*) Yes, of course, I'll make sure no one disturbs us, dear, if that's what you want. (*to herself*) This is a nightmare.

Neschast Excellent. (*He puts the handbell on the table and sits down on a chair next to it.*)

Gurmyz (*noticing her box on the table*) Oh, look, my box! I'd forgotten it. (*sweetly*) Be so kind as to pass me that box, would you, dear?

Neschast Don't worry! It's fine where it is.

Gurmyz Well, if you won't pass it, I'll get it myself.

Neschast (*taking out a pistol and putting it on the table*) Don't trouble yourself, Auntie.

Gurmyz (*alarmed*) Ah! There's nothing of value in there, you know. Just essential papers and – estate documents, that's all.

Neschast Really? (*opening the box*) Mind if I have a peep . . .?

Gurmyz Oh, dear God . . .

Neschast No, you're mistaken, Auntie, there's money in here. Bundles of it! The root of all evil, Auntie. We'd better close it up. (*Closes the box.*) There's this story of a provincial actor who was insulted by the wife of some producer. The actor said nothing but he never forgot the insult. The memory of it festered all winter. Just before the season finished the producer gave a farewell party for the actors. Are you listening, Auntie?

Gurmyz I'm listening.

Neschast At the end of the party, people begin saying their farewells and the actor approaches the hostess: 'Your hand, if I may,' he says. She gives it to him, Auntie, and he bites off one of her fingers!

Gurmyz Why are you telling me this?

Neschast Of course, he was a complete idiot. He could have gone about it a bit more subtly.

Gurmyz Is this relevant at all?

Neschast Just keep it in mind. Another actor, though, behaved far more intelligently. He was poor but with a noble heart, the nephew of a wealthy female landowner. And he took it into his head to visit his aunt whom he hadn't seen for fifteen years. When he eventually arrives, he's made very welcome. Then, all of a sudden, the aunt finds out he's an actor, and immediately she drives him out of the house without so much as a goodbye, humiliating him in front of everyone, in front of the servants.

Gurmyz Oh, no, Gennadiy . . .

Neschast However, it didn't turn out quite as she'd planned. For the actor concerned was Neschastlivtsev who refused to be trifled with. (*He opens the box.*) Firstly, Neschastlivtsev needed money for his journey. It wouldn't have been proper to have left his wealthy aunt's home on foot. (*He counts out some money.*) Then, he observed that his charitable aunt had a poor young girl living with her. And he thought, what use is this charity if it results in the wretched girl trying to drown herself?

Gurmyz What is all this nonsense?

Neschast Out of the goodness of his heart, he decided to take her with him. So we ought to put a bit aside for her keep. (*He counts out some more money.*) Then, there's the question of my own inheritance. I appreciate you won't be leaving me anything when you die – it'll all go to the infant prodigy – so I'll take something in lieu of that as well . . . (*He counts out more money.*)

Gurmyz Don't keep tormenting me. How much do you need?

Neschast Tell you what, I'll be magnanimous.

He rises, the pistol in one hand and the box in the other, which he gives to Gurmyzhskaya.

You give it to me yourself.

Gurmyz (*looking at the pistol*) This is farcical! I owe you a thousand roubles, anyway. Here! If you want any more, I'm prepared to –

Neschast (*taking the money*) No! There's no need for handouts. Thank you, Auntie. (*He puts the money away.*)

Gurmyz Would you please stop waving that pistol about, it's terrifying.

Neschast It's alright, you're perfectly safe. If things had got awkward, as a last resort I might have shot the sprog, but you've no need to worry. (*He puts the pistol away and rings the bell.*) Now, Auntie, why don't you give me a proper send off, eh? We'll have lunch, then exchange fond farewells, just like proper relatives.

Gurmyz Yes, of course.

Neschast I arrived here as a gentleman, I shall leave as a gentleman.

Enter Karp.

Karp, old boy, send someone into town as soon as possible to hire the best troika to take me to the nearest steamer jetty. And before I leave, old chap, the mistress wants you to organise the finest luncheon you can muster. And make sure there's champagne.

Karp Yes, sir. Lunch coming up!

Gurmyz Serve it in the dining room, Karp!

Neschast And call Arkadiy! (*to Gurmyzhskaya*) As a leaving present, I'll introduce you to Arkadiy. You'll find you haven't missed much –

Karp Ivan Petrovich and his son are waiting to see you, ma'am.

Gurmyz Show them into the dining room, I'll see them later.

Exit Karp.

Will you excuse me. I must get dressed. I'm expecting other guests. You go in the dining room. Have something before your journey. I'll look in to say goodbye.

Neschast We'll part friends? You're not angry with me?

Gurmyz No, I'm not angry. You could have behaved with a little more – decorum. After all, I am a woman . . .

Neschast Oh, God! I have offended you, haven't I? I knew it. I'll never forgive myself. I'll shoot myself here and now, Auntie. (*He takes out the pistol.*)

Gurmyz Ah, no, no!

Neschast Tell me! Tell me I offended you?

Gurmyz No, no, not at all! You didn't! No, no no!

She exits hurriedly.

Neschast (*calmly*) I'm glad to hear that. I can't make up my mind at the moment whether I'm Neschastlivtsev or Rothschild.

Enter Schastlivtsev.

Arkadiy, we're due for that holiday. I'm in the money, old chap. (*He waves the bundle of bank notes.*) You and I are heading for the Volga in the best available troika, and then first class on the steamer.

Schast Gennadiy Dem'yanych, you're a genius. Wonderful! I really do love luxury, you know.

Neschast If we get any decent offers of work, we'll take them. If we don't – to hell with it. When we get to Nizhniy next September, we'll give a performance at the festival with our new star, our new company. In the meantime, let's get pissed.

Schast You won't find a better drinking companion. This is the life I was born for. Poverty? Any fool can live in poverty, can't they? But to spend all that money with nothing to show for it, that takes real talent.

Neschast (*indicating the dining room*) Champagne, then? One for the road, one for each other and then another for – for the champagne.

Schast Excellent. You know, I'm a great supporter of rich people. Always have been. Show me a man who drinks champagne, smokes good cigars, and I'll show you a real man. The rest are nonentities. Don't you agree?

They both go off into the dining room. A burst of chatter from there. Aksyusha enters. She goes to the dining room door and peeps through, trying to attract someone's attention.

Aksyusha (*quietly, signalling*) Petya! Petya!

Pyotr enters swiftly from the dining room.

Pyotr Have you talked to him – ?

Aksyusha Quietly, for God's sake! Listen, it's no use. My cousin's got no money. I'm running away with him. Far away and for ever. It's either that or . . .

She takes his head in her hands and kisses it.

Good-bye! Go! Go!

Pyotr You're going away? Why?

Aksyusha I'm going on the stage. To be an actress.

Pyotr Have you gone mad?

Aksyusha It's decided. It's all settled. Go, please, go! Say goodbye now, my love, while we're alone. Not in front of everyone. That would be unbearable. Only follow me with your eyes, I'll keep looking at you . . .

Pyotr You can't do this. You can't. Listen, I've been talking to my dad again.

Aksyusha Well?

Pyotr He said he'd settle for a thousand, just to get rid of me. He's come down to a thousand, you see. We only need a thousand.

Aksyusha (*torn with indecision*) Oh, why didn't they let me drown?

Pyotr What?

Enter Neschastlivtsev.

Neschast Ah! I've found you!

Aksyusha Cousin, listen! There's still a ray of hope. Petya tells me his father only wants a thousand roubles now. Would you speak to my aunt again? Maybe she'll take pity on us. Just a thousand, that's all we need.

Neschast But what about your career as an actress, child? Harness those emotions of yours and we could . . .

Aksyusha (*tearfully*) Cousin, I need all my emotions just to get through my own life. I don't have any to spare.

Pyotr None at all.

Neschast Oh, vacillation! Vacillation!

> *Our doubts are traitors*
> *And make us lose the good we oft might win.*

Very well. Let's go back in. I'll first commune with the liquid muse and then I'll have another word with Auntie.

They go into the dining room.
Enter Milonov, Bodayev and Karp.

Karp The mistress will be with you in a moment, gentlemen.

Milonov What's going on here, Karp? There's a lot of activity.

Karp I couldn't say, sir.

Gurmyzhskaya enters, elegantly and youthfully dressed, on Bulanov's arm.

Gurmyz Do excuse me, gentlemen, for keeping you waiting.

Bodayev We weren't.

Milonov (*kissing her hand*) Ah, dear lady. As beautiful as ever. And you grow younger by the day.

Gurmyz I shall need to. Gentlemen, originally I invited you here, of course, to witness the signing of my will. However, circumstances have changed. I'm delighted to announce that I am to be married. May I present my future husband.

Milonov Oh, how marvellous.

Bodayev I guessed as much.

Gurmyz Please, everyone, do sit down.

Milonov and Bodayev sit.

Aleksis . . .

Bulanov Raisa, if you don't mind, I'd prefer to stand here beside you.

Gurmyz Isn't he wonderful? Gentlemen, I do hope you won't pre-judge me. I can see from your faces you may. But look at it from my point of view. I am vulnerable. A lone woman. The estate is going to ruin. As you may recall, I had hoped to pass it on to my nephew but I have just learnt – and I can tell you I am still reeling from this news, reeling – that he's a provincial actor . . .

Milonov Oh dear! How simply appalling.

Bodayev What is?

Milonov The news about her nephew.

Bodayev Don't ask me. I don't know anything about him.

Gurmyz He also leads a very dissolute life. He's still here, you can judge for yourselves. As for my niece, I'm afraid, she's proved equally disappointing. I am very displeased with her indeed. Anyway, I wanted you to know that, as a result, although I had always vowed to remain a widow, I am sacrificing myself for the good of the estate. To ensure it will not fall into the wrong hands.

Milonov What a selfless act. You're a heroine, ma'am.

Bodayev She's a what?

A burst of merriment from the dining room.

Gurmyz Gentlemen, we'll be taking a late luncheon to-day. Would you care to join me in a glass of champagne. Karp, fetch some from the dining room.

Another burst of laughter.

That's assuming there's any left.

Karp Yes, ma'am. May I also congratulate you, ma'am.

Gurmyz Thank you, Karp.

Karp goes into the dining room.

Milonov Of course, you should have done this a long time ago.

Gurmyz Ah, there was the little matter of finding the right man. And what a man he is. If only you knew. (*gazing tenderly at Bulanov*) Oh, my dear!

Bulanov Raisa! I'm quite embarrassed. Gentlemen, I shall try to prove myself worthy of the great honour that Raisa has bestowed upon me –

A roar from the dining room. Gurmyzhskaya frowns.

– as for her interests, I think you'll see within a very short time, gentlemen, how close those are to my own heart.

Karp returns with a tray of champagne glasses which he proceeds to pass round.

Let my actions speak for themselves. I promise you, this estate will shortly be flourishing again.

Milonov Oh, bravo, bravo!

Bulanov I can assure you I take very seriously my obligations, not merely to the estate, but to the community at large. Furthermore, I can promise, you will find in me an ardent defender of those rights and privileges which we all hold so dear.

Milonov Bravo! There speaks the younger generation . . .

Gurmyz You see what I mean . . .

Bodayev Nonsense. He'll squander the lot.

Milonov (*taking a glass*) Everything sublime and everything beautiful is founded on diversity, on contrast. Take the finest combinations in nature, and what do we find?

Cheering from the dining room.

Grim granite and melancholy ivy, indestructible oak and tender convolvulus. And now, before our eyes, unassailable virtue, worldly wisdom, tempered by experience, united with a tender, young sapling from a distinguished nursery.

Another cheer.

Raisa Pavlovna, Aleksey Sergeyevich! I wish you a long life, a serene life, a joyful life, the continuing support of your friends and the affec –

Another cheer.

– and the affection and loyalty from the –

A huge roar.

Gurmyz What on earth are they doing out there, Karp?

Karp They're drinking your health, ma'am. I took the liberty of telling them.

Gurmyz There is such a thing as moderation. (*to Milonov*) I'm sorry, do continue . . .

Milonov I'm afraid I am too moved to say any more.

Bodayev Jolly good.

Milonov I am so touched by your happiness. I find such happiness to be –

Gurmyz (*swiftly shaking Milonov's hand*) Thank you, thank you.

More cheers from the dining room.

Bodayev (*glass raised*) Congratulations! Do your best to live happily. I'll be delighted and amazed if you do! (*Drinks.*)

Gurmyz Thank you very much! (*to Bulanov*) What a coarse man!

From the dining room, a final cheer. Then the doors burst open and in comes Neschastlivtsev.
Schastlivtsev, Vosmibratov, Pyotr and Aksyusha remain by the doors.

Neschast Auntie, you're getting married? Congratulations! It's about time, about time! It'll do you a lot of good and it's nice for your relatives. Personally, I thoroughly approve of the union. You were made for each other.

(*Turns towards the doors.*) Gentlemen, why are you standing there!

    Schastlivtsev and Vosmibratov step forward.

Auntie, may I introduce my good friend, Arkadiy Schastlivtsev!

Gurmyz Delighted!

Milonov So this is your nephew.

Neschast (*to Milonov*) May I have the honour to introduce myself? Gennadiy Gurmyzhskiy. (*to Bodayev*) Gurmyzhskiy, Gennadiy!

    Milonov and Bodayev get up, shake hands and sit down.

Vosmib (*to Gurmyzhskaya*) Very pleased for you, ma'am. All legal and proper as it should be. I'm delighted.

Gurmyz And what do you think of my fiancé, Ivan Petrovich?

Vosmib Not bad, ma'am, as bridegrooms go, ma'am. And you never know, he'll probably get brighter the older he gets.

Neschast (*to Schastlivtsev and Vosmibratov*) Gentlemen, please do sit down. Auntie, if you'll allow me, I'll be host for a moment. Karp, old chap, could you dig us out a nice bottle of wine, a good vintage, nothing cheap. It's not every year Auntie gets married.

    He sits down. Schastlivtsev and Vosmibratov do likewise.
    Karp exits.

I'm sorry, gentlemen, carry on with your conversation, we won't interrupt.

Milonov No, please. We'd love to hear from you, wouldn't we?

Gurmyz No, I think we're –

Neschast Well, if you insist, with the greatest of pleasure, gentlemen. I always enjoy conversing in such distinguished circles. Auntie, you're a very fortunate woman, aren't you?

Gurmyz Yes, my dear, I am fortunate.

Neschast It's said, people who enjoy good fortune become kinder and nobler. Isn't that so, gentlemen?

Milonov Absolutely true!

Neschast Auntie, you have a niece, a dear, gentle creature who also has a suitor. He isn't as handsome or as fearless as yours. Or as young. But she loves him. And this is his dad.

Gurmyz I know, my dear.

Neschast Now his dad is at first glance a God-fearing, law-abiding Russian gentleman, who adores his children and who likes nothing better than to marry off his sons. In truth, out of sheer greed and ignorance, he will only sell his sons for thousand rouble dowries. Isn't that the case, my friend?

Vosmib Absolutely true, squire. As a wise man once said, business is business.

Neschast Auntie, here is a golden opportunity for you to play the fairy godmother.

Gurmyz No, no, no. Now you stop that, at once. You mustn't interfere, it has nothing to do with you. Besides, I've already spent vast sums, and I have enormous expenses ahead.

Bulanov Raisa and I can't spend on anything unnecessary now. I have plans to set up a stud farm and then there are ponds to be cleared, ditches to be dug . . .

Neschast Are you refusing to give anything?

Gurmyz I know it's not a huge sum in itself, but you must understand, gentlemen, that currently . . .

Neschast It needn't be cash. In present company, your word is quite sufficient . . .

Vosmib As far as I'm concerned, ma'am, your spoken word is a written contract.

Gurmyz No, no, I'm sorry! This is not something we can discuss publicly in front of strangers. I'm being unfairly coerced . . .

Bulanov Raisa, you must categorically refuse.

Gurmyz Gentlemen, you must surely see that I can't – I can't suddenly – like that! No, I categorically refuse.

Neschast I see. (*to Vosmibratov*) Come on then, old chap. I appeal to you. Can't you bring the price down a bit? Just this once?

Vosmib I couldn't do that. I come down as it is. That's only as a favour, because she's from a good home . . .

Neschast Auntie, Raisa Pavlovna! Benefactress of all humanity! Don't allow yourself to be discredited in front of this honourable company! Don't shame the family name of Gurmyzhskiy. I'm embarrassed for you. After all, you've only got two relatives – me and her. She's not asking for much and I don't need a dowry. How can you refuse her such a sum? You're a rich woman, you wouldn't even miss it! Whereas I'm a penniless artist but I swear to you, if I had it . . . What am I talking about? I do have it. (*Takes the money out of his pocket.*) What the hell? I'll stay sober for a month.

Schast (*grasping his arm*) What on earth are you doing?

Neschast Quiet, Arkashka! (*to Gurmyzhskaya*) You really won't give her anything?

Gurmyz I'm sorry, no. I've already said so.

Neschast Well, if the rich landowner refuses the poor girl, the poor artist won't. (*to Aksyusha*) Come here, my child.

Schast But you promised we could go on a troika! There goes our troika! There goes our steamer.

Neschast Shut up, Arkashka!

Aksyusha approaches.

Here you are, my dear! Take it!

Aksyusha What are you doing, cousin? You don't have to do this, you know.

Neschast I said, take it! Once I've made up my mind, that's it.

Aksyusha (*embracing him*) Oh, cousin, dearest cousin!

Karp enters with a bottle of wine and glasses and puts them on the table.

Neschast Well, that's enough of that. Or else I'll start crying and get thoroughly embarrassing.

Aksyusha How can I thank you?

Neschast How can you thank me? What about saying thank you? That'll do. Now, let's have a drink!

He goes to the table and pours two glasses.
Aksyusha gives the money to Pyotr.

Pyotr (*giving the money to his father*) Here.

Vosmib Thank you, son.

Vosmibratov counts the money.

Gurmyz (*to Neschastlivtsev*) I must say, it's extraordinarily generous of you.

Neschast Glad you approve. Come here, Arkadiy, have a drink!

Schastlivtsev takes a glass and drinks.

Gurmyz (*to Aksyusha*) I'm delighted things have turned out for you so well, my dear. If there's any way I can help, just call on me. And come the wedding day, I want you to know I'll be more than happy to stand in for the mother you never really had.

Aksyusha bows.

Milonov (*approaching the table*) Congratulations, sir. A magnificent gesture. I'll make sure your generosity is reported in full in the newspaper.

Neschast I don't give a stuff about the newspapers. Let's get drunk!

Milonov My dear sir, we can't possibly do that. Not here.

Neschast If you don't want to, clear off. I don't care. Arkadiy, let me fill your glass.

Milonov moves away.

Bodayev (*to Bulanov*) Who is that chap?

Bulanov He's an actor –

Bodayev An actor? Good gracious! Bravo, bravo! (*to Neschastlivtsev*) Your hand, sir! I was wondering who it was speaking so clearly, with such integrity. It's rare enough round these parts. (*indicating Schastlivtsev*) Is he an actor as well?

Neschast Yes, he's an actor.

Bodayev What sort of things does he do?

Schast I do birdsong impersonations.

Bodayev Really? Jolly good! Jolly good! Never seen it, I'm afraid. (*to Neschastlivtsev*) Remind me. I'll give him a meerschaum pipe as a present. And, both of you, feel free to call on me at any time.

Neschast What, so we can entertain you for free? Bugger off!

Bodayev (*bellowing with laughter*) What? That's very funny!

Neschast More wine.

Bodayev moves away.

Gurmyz (*to Bulanov*) We've got to get rid of him somehow. God knows what he'll do next.

Bulanov Listen, old man, time you were getting ready to leave, surely?

Neschast I've been getting ready for a long time, shrimp.

Bulanov Well, I think it's time for you to go now.

Neschast Arkadiy, they're kicking us out. The interesting question is, why on earth did we call here in the first place? How did we get into this forest, crawl into this undergrowth? See what we've done? We've disturbed the wild life, old chap. Frightened all the birds of prey. Upset the natural order. Where old ladies marry schoolboys and young girls drown because life's so unbearable. That's the forest for you. Come on, let's creep away. Leave them be.

Gurmyz (*shrugging her shoulders*) Clowns.

Neschast Clowns? We are artists, ma'am, artists. You are the clowns. Us? If we love, then we love; if we don't love, then we quarrel and fight. If we offer help, we give it right down to our last half-kopeck. But you? All your lives you talk about social welfare, about loving your fellow men. And what have you done? Who have you ever comforted or consoled? Who have you ever provided for, apart from yourselves? You're the clowns, the fools, not us. When I have money, I share it with layabouts like Arkashka here, whilst my own aunt is having a hard time feeding me for two days. A young girl goes and tries to drown herself. Who truly pushed her into the water? You, Auntie. And who rescued her? The actor, Neschastlivtsev! *Oh you people! You people! You breed of crocodiles with your sham tears! Your hearts of steel! Your kisses that fly like daggers to the heart! Lions and leopards feed their own children, birds of prey care for their young, whilst she . . . she! Where is love? Where is love to be found here? Oh, if only I were a wolf. I'd set about these heartless forest rodents and tear them limb from limb!*

Milonov You can be held accountable for talk like that, you know!

Bulanov Yes, send for the police. We're all witnesses!

Neschast (*to Milonov*) Me? Accountable? I beg your pardon, I think you're under a misapprehension. Not me. (*producing a playscript from his pocket*) Schiller's *The Robbers*. Look! Passed by the censor for public performance. You pathetic little man. I can't think why I even deign to speak to you. I talk like Schiller and you – like a government pencil-pusher! Enough! Let's go, Arkashka! Good-bye! (*Bows to them all.*) Auntie, your hand, please!

Gurmyz (*hiding her hand in panic*) Oh, no, no . . .

Bulanov Let him, Raisa. The sooner you do, the sooner he'll be gone . . .

Neschast Don't be afraid, I'm not going to bite it off.

Milonov Of course he won't bite it off.

Bulanov Of course not . . .

Gurmyz Oh, no, you don't know!

Neschast Oh, people, people!

He puts on his knapsack. Aksyusha helps him and kisses him. He picks up his stick.

Well, Arkadiy, you and I have had a feast, we've made a bit of noise, now it's back to work again! Listen, Karp! If a troika comes, you send it back to the town, old chap. Say that the gentlemen have gone ahead on foot. Your arm, my friend! (*linking arms with Schastlivtsev, as they go*)

Forever, and forever, farewell, Cassius!
If we do meet again, why, we shall smile;
If not, why then this parting was well made . . .

As they walk out together –
  Curtain.